THE ROAD TO COMMUNISM

THE ROAD TO COMMUNISM

TED GOTTFRIED

THE RISE AND FALL OF THE SOVIET UNION

ILLUSTRATED BY MELANIE REIM

TWENTY-FIRST CENTURY BOOKS
BROOKFIELD, CONNECTICUT

Photographs courtesy of Underwood Archives, S.F.: p. 19; Brown Brothers: p. 23; Hulton Getty/Archive Photos: pp. 28, 60, 65, 74, 88, 119, 121; Culver Pictures, Inc.: p. 41; The Illustrated London News: pp. 99, 108. Map by Joe LeMonnier

Library of Congress Cataloging-in-Publication Data
Gottfried, Ted.
The road to Communism / Ted Gottfried.
p. cm. – (The Rise and fall of the Soviet Union)
Includes bibliographical references and index.
Summary: Chronicles the Czarist Russian Empire in the 1800s, the birth of Bolshevism, events leading to the Russian Revolution of 1917, and the development of new political structures in its aftermath.
ISBN 0-7613-2557-3 (lib. bdg.)
1. Soviet Union—History—Revolution, 1917-1921—Juvenile literature. [1. Soviet Union—History—Revolution, 1917-1921.] I. Title.
DK189 . G68 2002   957'.07—dc21   2001052252

Published by Twenty-First Century Books
A Division of The Millbrook Press, Inc.
2 Old New Milford Road
Brookfield, Connecticut 06804
www.millbrookpress.com

DEDICATION

For Rudy Kornmann,
computer whiz,
with much thanks
for all the help over the years

ACKNOWLEDGMENTS

I am grateful to personnel of the New York Central Research Library, the Mid-Manhattan Library, and the Society Library in New York City for aid in gathering material for this book. Thanks are also due my friend George Fried for his loan of the 1911 classic edition of the *Encyclopaedia Britannica Handy Volume Issue,* an invaluable research tool. Also, gratitude and much love to my wife, Harriet Gottfried, who—as always—read and critiqued this book. Her help was invaluable, but any shortcomings in the work are mine alone.

Ted Gottfried

CONTENTS

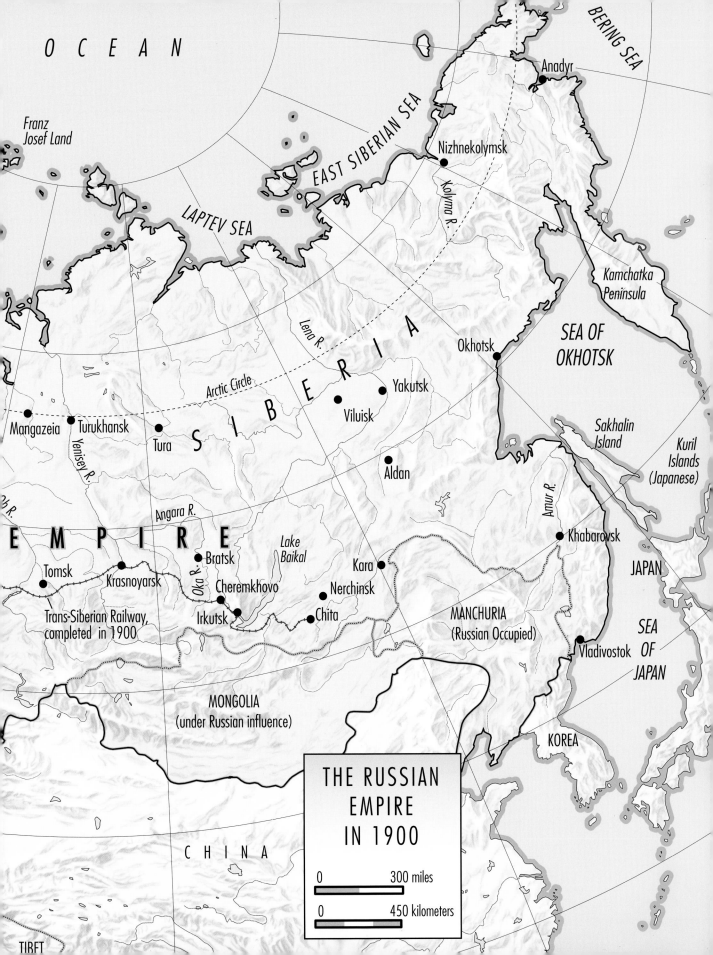

OCEAN

Franz
Josef Land

LAPTEV SEA

EAST SIBERIAN SEA

BERING SEA

Anadyr

Nizhnekolymsk

Kolyma R.

Kamchatka
Peninsula

SEA OF
OKHOTSK

Okhotsk

Lena R.

Arctic Circle

S I B E R I A

Yakutsk

Viluisk

Mangazeia   Turukhansk

Yenisey R.

Tura

Aldan

Sakhalin
Island

Kuril
Islands
(Japanese)

Ob R.

E M P I R E

Angara R.

Lake
Baikal

Amur R.

Khabarovsk

JAPAN

Tomsk

Krasnoyarsk

Bratsk

Oka R.

Cheremkhovo

Irkutsk

Kara

Nerchinsk

Chita

MANCHURIA
(Russian Occupied)

Vladivostok

SEA
OF
JAPAN

Trans-Siberian Railway,
completed in 1900

MONGOLIA
(under Russian influence)

KOREA

CHINA

THE RUSSIAN
EMPIRE
IN 1900

0	300 miles

0	450 kilometers

TIBET

PREFACE

History is too often a sad story. One of the saddest is that of the rise and fall of the Soviet Union. The key political development of the twentieth century, it is a saga that spans nine decades from the reign of Nicholas II, the last tsar of Imperial Russia, to the fall of Mikhail Gorbachev, the last Communist ruler of the Union of Soviet Socialist Republics (USSR). It is a history that not only transformed Russia but also had an ongoing effect on many other countries of the world.

This book deals with the start of that history: how oppression stirred rebellion, how words inspired violence, and how in the end violence betrayed the words and spawned oppression. It covers the Russian Revolution, the tyranny that caused it, and the terror of communism that followed. It is the chronicle of a dream that failed, of an idealistic vision turned to ashes.

EMPIRE OF
THE TSARS

> **Wretched and abundant,**
> **Oppressed and powerful,**
> **Weak and mighty,**
> **Mother Russia!**
>
> *from* **Who Is Happy in Russia?**
> by nineteenth-century
> Russian poet Nikolai Nekrasov

Peasants called it *Mother Russia.* Aristocrats called it *Imperial Russia.* Its royal family of emperors, the Romanovs, called it *Tsarist Russia.* It was Russia in the late nineteenth and early twentieth centuries, Russia before the revolution, Russia before the Communists ruled. It was the empire that the industrialized world had left behind, a realm stalled in time, an agricultural society in the early stages of developing the mills and factories that had been producing wealth in most of the nations of Europe and the United States for almost a hundred years. It was a land of contradictions, of grinding poverty and opulent wealth, of long-suffering peasants and upper-class revolutionaries; of corrupt secret police and idealistic assassins, of wily mystics and gullible royalty.

THE EMANCIPATION OF THE SERFS

The Imperial Russian Empire extended "over a vast territory in E. [eastern] Europe and N. [northern] Asia with an area exceeding 8,660,000 sq. m., or one-sixth of the land surface of the globe."[1] It stretched from the Baltic and Barents seas and Bering Strait in the north to Afghanistan and China in the south, and from the borders of the German and Austro-Hungarian empires, and the Black Sea in the west, to the Bering Sea and the Sea of Japan in the east. The Russian Empire included Finland, Poland, the Ukraine, Turkestan, and Siberia, as well as the vast area then known as European Russia.[2] It spanned the continents of Europe and Asia.

In 1906 the population of Imperial Russia was 149,299,300.[3] It was "a country four-fifths of whose population consisted of peasants."[4] Before 1861 these peasants had been serfs who toiled for large landowners or on government-owned land. Serfs lived in the most primitive conditions, had few rights under the law, and were virtually slaves. In 1861, Tsar Alexander II, who ruled from 1855 to 1881, issued an emancipation proclamation, which freed the serfs.

Presumably, they "were liberated entirely from the . . . rule of the landowners," and now owned the land themselves.[5] Actually, it wasn't that simple. The Imperial Russian government had bought the estates from the owners and sold the land to the peasants through a mortgage arrangement, which required the peasants to pay the government back over a period of years. In addition to the mortgage, there was interest to be paid, as well as taxes. The system kept many of the peasants from actually attaining full ownership of the land.

Nevertheless, many peasants initially regarded the tsars — Alexander II and his successors — as their protectors against the cruel oppression of the landowning aristocracy. Over the next fifty years, however, that attitude slowly changed. Most Russian farmlands were lush and the produce plentiful, but the transportation system was undeveloped; too often the food could not be moved to markets before it spoiled. The peasants had no experience in managing their land or marketing their produce. They had few contacts among middlemen and retailers. Historians would record that "the economic and moral condition of the peasantry was little improved by freedom, and in many districts there were signs of positive impoverishment and demoralization."[6] There were also periods of widespread starvation.

Local governments of small farming communities were overseen by the tsar's secret police. They intruded into many aspects of the peasants' lives. Village politics were monitored by the secret police to prevent radical influences. A constant watch was kept on the selling of produce and the buying of goods to prevent cheating the tax collector. Worst of all, both the secret police and the local governments were corrupt, and this corruption was a constant burden to the peasants. Payoffs to local officials were an ongoing drain on their meager finances.

A RADICAL DEFECT

The landowners had "received good money for the (often inferior) land." However, they had been "deprived of the free labour of the serfs and their tools and animals." The owners had little knowledge of the business world and considered it beneath their station to work for a living. Nevertheless, they "went on spending in the same old lavish way, furnishing their manor houses in the French Empire style and sending their sons to the most expensive schools."[7]

By the late 1880s many of the landowners had gone deeply into debt. Since they were aristocrats with ties to the fabulously wealthy tsars, their debts were carried by banks, moneylenders, and others who extended them credit. It followed that they were the most loyal subjects that the monarchy had. It puzzled them that so many of their university-educated offspring became radicals determined to bring down the monarchy. They did not understand, as their children did, that the tsarist regime was cruel and oppressive, that its policies kept the Russian people from improving their lot the way people in the industrialized nations of the world had, and that those policies were increasingly isolating Russia from the rest of Europe.

During the final years of the nineteenth century, many revolutionary movements had sprung up in Russia, mostly in the larger cities. There were periodic riots, and frequent assassination attempts on prominent noblemen in the government, and on members of the royal family, including the tsars. Some of these attempts were successful.

The various revolutionary groups behind the violence were made up mostly of young intellectuals whom Tsar Nicholas II, who ruled from 1895 to 1918, called "intelligentsia," making "the same face as when pronouncing the word 'syphilis.'"[8] Aside from being activists, they were thinkers and debaters. They could not agree among themselves, and so they could not act together with the singleness of purpose needed to organize peasants and workers to topple the tsarist regime.

AN ASSASSINATION PLOT

On March 1, 1887, five students at St. Petersburg University were arrested by the tsarist secret police for plotting to assassinate Nicholas's father, Tsar Alexander III, ruler of the Imperial Russian Empire from 1881 to 1894. On that same date, six years earlier, the previous tsar, Alexander II, had been killed by a terrorist bomb. The sentence of death on Alexander II had been passed by a small, secret organization calling itself Narodnaia Volia (People's Will). "The stated mission of the People's Will," according to Professor Richard Pipes in his book *The Russian Revolution,* "was to assassinate government officials, for the twin goal of demoralizing the government and breaking down the awe in which the masses held the Tsar."[9] The five students accused in the second assassination plot were also followers of People's Will.

When arrested for the second plot, one of the students was carrying a bomb. Although the activists of People's Will considered themselves leaderless, the tsarist authorities identified the bomb carrier as the leader of the group. His name was Alexander Ulianov.

As a student, Alexander Ulianov's main interest had been science. During his first three years at St. Petersburg University, he had shown no interest in politics. During his fourth year he was introduced to theories of social democracy, and then to Marxism. This led him to the ultraviolent movement of People's Will. Alexander accepted their doctrine that "members were expected to dedicate themselves totally to the revolutionary cause, and if called upon, to sacrifice to it their properties and even their lives."[10]

The year before he and his four comrades were arrested, Alexander Ulianov's father had died suddenly of a cerebral hemorrhage. He left behind a wife and six children—three boys and three girls—of whom Alexander was the oldest. The family was devastated when Alexander was tried and convicted, and then hanged publicly along with his four co-conspirators.

A BROTHER'S LEGACY

One of the brothers he left behind was seventeen-year-old Vladimir Ilich Ulianov. He and Alexander had not been particularly close. Indeed, Alexander had often criticized "Vladimir's rude manners and habitual sneer." Also, young Vladimir "showed no interest in public affairs." However, that would change as he grew older. He would also change his last name from Ulianov to Lenin—a name that over the years would be hailed by some and feared by many.[11]

Lenin was born on April 10, 1870, in Simbirsk, Russia. His father was a tsarist bureaucrat and educator who had risen to become a nobleman. Lenin's mother, of German ancestry, was the daughter of a doctor. By the standards of the times, the home in which Lenin grew up was upper class.

After graduating from high school with honors, Lenin enrolled as a law student at Kazan University. Here he was recognized as the brother of a martyred revolutionary and welcomed into radical student circles. After participating in a violent demonstration, he was expelled. However, he was allowed to continue his studies on his own. In 1891 he passed his examinations and became an attorney. Over the next few years Lenin was strongly influenced by the theories of the German Communist Karl Marx. He was also drawn to the writings of Nicholas Chernyshevsky, who called upon opponents of the tsarist regime in Russia to dedicate their lives to taking revolutionary action against it.

In 1893, Lenin relocated to St. Petersburg, the capital city of Imperial Russia. Although young, he was already going bald, and as if to compensate he grew a distinctive pointed Vandyke beard. These physical characteristics were much used in political cartoons drawn of him in later years when he became a prominent figure on the world stage. In St. Petersburg, Lenin became more deeply involved in radical activities. In the Marxist movement he met Nadezhda Krupskaya, and they became romantically involved. Along with others in their circle, Nadezhda was impressed with Lenin's single-minded devotion to the cause of revolution. Always serious, and somewhat humorless, Lenin was called *Starik,* "the old one," by his associates.[12]

Vladimir Lenin

HE WHO FIGHTS AND RUNS AWAY . . .

Arrested for revolutionary activity in 1895, Lenin was sent to prison, and then exiled to Siberia. Nadezhda joined him there, and they were married in 1898. Two years later, upon their release, the couple fled to Switzerland. Lenin plunged back into the Marxist movement and in 1902 wrote a pamphlet entitled *What Is to Be Done?* It had a major impact on the Second Congress of Russian Social Democrats held in London in 1903.

The key issue at the congress was party organization and membership. Lenin pointed out that the dissatisfactions of workers would always be defused by better wages and working conditions. A revolutionary movement, he said, could not depend on them. It would have to "consist of professional full-time revolutionaries." He also called for "a Russian revolutionary movement that included the peasantry." To committed Marxists, this was a brazen denial of Marx's belief that the peasants were "a conservative force who would stand in the way of revolution."[13]

When rebellion broke out in Russia in 1905, Lenin returned to his homeland, arriving in early November. The following month he helped to rally forces for an uprising in Moscow. What followed was the first example of the cowardice Lenin would always be accused of by his critics. It was reported that "as soon as the shooting began he made himself scarce."[14] The following day he fled to Finland. He returned after the uprising had been crushed, but quickly left for Switzerland. Lenin did not return to Russia again until 1917 when revolution was no longer an idealistic dream, but rather a bloody and chaotic reality.

A HELPLESS GIANT

Lenin was thirty-five years old during the 1905 rebellion. Seemingly, it had proved him wrong and Marx right when it came to rallying the peasants for revolution. Because the empire was so vast, and distances so great, it had been impossible to organize the peasants into any kind of supporting force to bring down the government. For the same reasons, although the misery of the peasants was mounting, their rumblings of discontent were muted by the time they reached the ears of the rulers in St. Petersburg.

Many of the peasants had much to complain about. Wheat production was affected by the soil erosion caused by outmoded planting techniques and lack of modern farming equipment. The hovels in which the peasants lived were falling apart for lack of income to repair them. Crops were rotting in the fields because frequent breakdowns of the archaic Russian railway system prevented transporting them to market. Taxes and mortgage payments were an ongoing burden.

To add to it all, the backbreaking labor of picking crops could not be done by those most able, the strong young men who by Russian law had to serve five to six years in the army. Boasting "a standing army of 2.6 million men, Russia had the largest military establishment in the world." However, it lacked mobility. "Great distances aggravated by an inadequate railroad network" rendered troops unavailable for battle when an enemy struck. In effect, the Russian army was a helpless giant.[15]

INTERNATIONAL ANARCHISTS

If a major revolution erupted in the early 1900s, the army, which was mostly strung out along Russia's borders, could not be depended upon to stop it. However, Tsar Nicholas II, and particularly Tsarina Alexandra, his wife, did not believe that revolution was possible. They saw themselves as beloved monarchs whom the Russian people adored. They regarded the peasants as their children, perhaps naughty at times, but at heart loving their imperial parents. They were also deaf to the complaints of the exploited and downtrodden factory workers and miners who were, in any case, too few in numbers for their grievances to impress the royal couple.

What did frighten the rulers, however, were the student radicals who were close at hand in St. Petersburg, Moscow, and other major Russian cities. Their voices were loud and their actions were violent. The memory of the assassination of Alexander II and the attempt on the life of Alexander III were still fresh in their minds at the turn of the century. One never knew when the disciples of People's Will might strike again.

People's Will was a Russian version of anarchism, a worldwide movement that proposed that heads of state should be assassinated on the theory that this would cause the collapse of the repressive governments they led. The movement decreed that anarchists themselves should be leaderless, and that individuals acting on their own, or in small cells (groups), should carry out acts of rebellion against the state, including assassination.

On five occasions between 1894 and 1901, anarchists had committed such acts. They had assassinated President Sadi Carnot of France in 1894, Premier Antonio Canovas of Spain in 1897, Empress Elizabeth of Austria in 1898, King Humbert of Italy in 1900, and President William McKinley of the United States in 1901.[16] Although not connected to the anarchist movement, People's Will copied their techniques.

What stood between any Russian assassins and Tsar Nicholas II and his family in Russia was the secret police. A department of the Ministry of the Interior and provided with unlimited funds, the secret police "dominated the whole ministry." Dmitrii Sergeevich Sipiagin, the minister of the interior, was in reality the head of the secret police. Their mission was to uncover plots against the regime and to apprehend the plotters. In effect, the tsarist secret police carried out "a hideous reign of terror" that "spread all over Russia." In practice, they were rarely responsible to anyone but themselves.[17]

THE INDIFFERENT TSAR

So long as they kept him alive, and kept any revolutionaries at bay, the turn-of-the-century tsar did not interfere with the secret police. Nor was Tsar Nicholas much interested in other matters of state. One historian describes him as "a narrow, rather dull-witted young man of no vision." A prominent church official of the period, the Chief Procurator of the Holy Synod, observed that the worldview of Nicholas II reflected "the influence of the many chambermaids who surround his mother." In a letter he wrote to his mother, Nicholas commented that "many strange things happen in the world. One reads about them and shrugs one's shoulders."[18]

Nicholas was twenty-seven years old in 1894 when his father, Alexander III, died unexpectedly, and he succeeded him as tsar. On the day of Nicholas's coronation, 500,000 people crowded into Khodynka Field outside Moscow to view the ceremonies. A riot ensued. It quickly turned to panic. Nearly 1,400 people were trampled to death. The tragedy did not stop the new tsar and his wife, Tsarina Alexandra, from leading the dancing at the Coronation Ball that evening.

Alexandra had been married to Nicholas for only one year when she became tsarina. She was four years younger than he, the daughter of a

The Romanov family,
about 1905: Tsar Nicholas II and Tsarina Alexandra
and their children, Tsarevich Alexis (on the tsarina's
lap), and Grand Duchesses (from left to right)
Tatiana, Marie, Anastasia, and Olga.

German prince, and the granddaughter of Queen Victoria of Great Britain. Born and raised in Germany, she was not popular in Russia, and behind her back was usually referred to as "the German woman." She was a snobbish young aristocrat, "haughty and cold," and alienated virtually everybody but her husband, who adored her. She had tremendous influence over him; some said she dominated him; through him she became a force to be reckoned with in Russian politics. She also "had a strong inclination to mysticism," a gullible faith in the powers of the occult.[19]

THE ROYAL DISEASE

Between 1895 and 1903, Alexandra gave birth to four daughters. In 1904 a son, Alexis, was born. Now there was a tsarevich, an heir to the throne of Imperial Russia. But there was a serious problem. Alexis had hemophilia, a disease that can be life threatening. Alexandra feared it would "imperil the future of the dynasty."[20]

People with hemophilia bleed easily and often. It is a disease "transmitted solely by females," and in the case of Alexis by his mother, the tsarina. The *Encyclopedia Britannica* points out that "its existence in certain royal families of Europe is well-known."[21] The reason is that intermarriage among these families, including the tsarist family of Imperial Russia, was common for centuries. One way or another, Alexandra and Nicholas were related to the queen of England, the kaiser of Germany, the kings of Sweden, Belgium, Greece, and Spain, the queen of Denmark, and the royal houses of Romania and Yugoslavia. Kings married princesses, queens married princes, and down the line their descendants bled.

Episodes of bleeding were an ongoing problem for little Alexis. The doctors seemed unable to put a stop to them. The tsarina was frantic. She sought spiritual help. She found it in one who professed to be a holy man from Siberia. Their meeting would have a profound effect on future events in Imperial Russia. The name the tsarina's spiritual adviser was known by was Rasputin.

He was also called the "mad monk."[22]

TURMOIL AND TERROR

Rasputin was a peasant who could neither read nor write. He had been born Grigory Yefimovich Novykh around 1872. He grew up in Pokrovskoye, a village in western Siberia, the son of a "relatively wealthy peasant family." Nevertheless, Grigory was remembered as "a dirty and unruly boy." As a young man, he acquired a reputation in the village as "a drunkard, a lecher and a horse thief." This led to the villagers giving him the name Rasputin, which meant "dissolute" or "debauched one."[1]

CHARLATAN OR HEALER?

Still in his youth, Rasputin joined a group of pilgrims bound for a monastery at Verkhoturye. He stayed there for three months, and gave up eating meat and drinking alcohol. At Verkhoturye he encountered the Khlysty, a mystical sect whose members "danced naked" and performed "group sex."[2] Rasputin was inspired to fashion his own doctrine "that the best means of salvation is to indulge one's appetites as much as possible."[3]

In 1903, Rasputin went to St. Petersburg. He was soon accepted by the aristocracy, who were caught up in a wave of spiritualism, which ran the gamut from seances and ouija boards to pagan cults and free love. Rasputin gained prominence as "a sinner and repentant, who had been graced with extraordinary powers of clairvoyance and healing."[4]

He stood out in the opulence of the nobility. The filthiness of the peasant blouse and baggy trousers he wore contrasted with the glittering chandeliers and diamond tiaras. His long hair and scraggly beard offended, yet attracted, the aristocrats. His breath was foul, his hands and bare feet unwashed, his body odor "compared to that of a goat."[5] He sometimes behaved like a country bumpkin. Nevertheless, Rasputin had charisma. His piercing blue eyes had a magnetic effect. There were reports of infidelities, affairs, and orgies involving him. It was said that participants had been hypnotized by Rasputin.

Although not a monk as he claimed, Rasputin earned a reputation as a healer. Even those who thought him a charlatan could not deny that he got results. It was this mysterious power that resulted in his being recommended to the tsarina in 1905 as one who might help the infant tsarevich's hemophilia.

Various theories have been offered as to why Rasputin was successful in halting Alexis's bleeding. Rasputin himself said that he "sometimes used Tibetan drugs or whatever else came to hand, and that sometimes he merely pretended to use remedies or mumbled nonsensical words while he prayed." Nevertheless, he brought under control the internal bleeding that the doctors had failed to stop. Both Alexandra and Tsar Nicholas accepted Rasputin's mystical powers as proof "that a simple Russian peasant who was close to God should be able to do what was beyond all the doctors."[6] They took it as a sign confirming their special relationship to the peasants who loved and were loyal to them. Rasputin increased his influence over them by bolstering this self-delusion at every opportunity. In 1905, however, that royal delusion was about to be shattered.

THE RELENTLESS HENCHMAN

Three years earlier, in April 1902, the head of the secret police and Minister of the Interior, Dimitrii Sergeevich Sipiagin, had been assassinated by a student radical. The tsar granted the police new and unlimited powers, and appointed Viacheslav Plehve as Sipiagin's successor. Plehve instituted a policy by which "Russia came close to becoming a police state."[7]

Grigory Rasputin
(second from left), surrounded by some
of his wealthy female followers

Plehve was the son of a German family, which had settled in Warsaw, Poland (then part of the Russian Empire), where he had been raised. After becoming a lawyer, in 1881 he had been appointed Director of the Department of Police. The department's mission was to fight any anti-tsarist activities. For the next twenty years Plehve had directed programs of political counterintelligence. He originated techniques of infiltration of revolutionary parties and was successful in destroying some of them. However, he made no distinction between moderate opposition groups and revolutionary ones. Any organization that criticized the tsar, or his government, was apt to be brutally crushed by Plehve.

Violently anti-Semitic, Plehve "made no secret of his dislike of Jews."[8] He blamed them for the revolutionary unrest plaguing Russia. He devised a propaganda campaign to convince the peasants that the Jews were responsible for their hardships. His agents spread the word through rural Russia that the revolutionaries were really tools of Jewish bankers out to bring down the tsar so they could seize control of the country.

THE KISHINEV POGROM

This outlandish claim that Jewish radicals and Jewish bankers were working hand in hand in a scheme that aimed to control and enslave Russia and eventually the world did not originate with Plehve. It was part of a document called *The Protocols of the Learned Elders of Zion*, written by a monk named Sergei Nilus. Published in 1903, it had been commissioned by Tsar Nicholas II. Pogroms—raids in which peasants and ruthless Russian cavalry units called Cossacks robbed, raped, and murdered Jews—had long been a fact of life in Russia. Recently, however, it had become "increasingly difficult to convince the ignorant Russian peasants of the necessity to kill innocent Jews in order to alleviate their own miserable condition." The tsar assigned Nilus "to come up with something to damn the Jews" anew.[9]

Actually, Jews were only a small minority in the many Russian reform movements. Also, a very few of the banks to which Imperial Russia owed money were owned by Jews. That financiers and radicals were in cahoots was an idea repugnant to both, and just plain silly on the face of it. Nevertheless, Plehve's agents did their work well. *The Protocols* were read aloud to gatherings of villagers. Old prejudices were stirred up. The peasants' discontent was successfully redirected toward the Jews. On April 16, 1903, a terrible pogrom erupted in the city of Kishinev.

Kishinev had a population of 100,000. Half of them were Jews. On Easter morning, "handbills appeared throughout Kishinev announcing that the tsar had granted permission to local Christians to wreak 'bloody punishment' upon Jews." It was preceded by months of rumors circulated by Plehve's agents that a Christian boy had been "killed by Jews who needed his blood to prepare for the Passover feast." The peasants of Kishinev were a downtrodden people, but they were also ignorant and bigoted. They had long believed that the Jewish religion required satanic rites. When a Christian girl died the night before Easter, new rumors touched off the pogrom, although the Jews had nothing to do with her death.[10]

Accounts of the Kishinev pogrom confirm that "scores of Jews . . . were savagely murdered. . . . Military officials were present, but did not try to stop the frenzied peasants as they raped and murdered. It is believed that the pogrom was incited by government officials."[11]

When news of the pogrom reached the United States, there was outrage. President Theodore Roosevelt sent a protest to the tsar condemning Russia's treatment of Jews. Nicholas was defiant. He rejected Roosevelt's plea that the persecution of Jews stop. Instead, with the help of Plehve, the tsar stepped up the campaign against the Jews. He issued an edict that said that Jews could only own property in their homes. This meant they were forbidden to own businesses, stores, land, or even horses or other livestock if it was stabled elsewhere.

Between 1903 and 1906, "a chain reaction of pogroms and mass expulsions threatened Russian Jewry's sheer physical survival."[12] During the early twentieth century there were a little more than five million Jews in Imperial Russia.[13] By 1917 more than a third had left. One and a half million Russian Jews had emigrated to the United States.[14]

WAR BREAKS OUT

If the tsar and Plehve had successfully used the Jews to defuse the peasants' unrest, they still had the student revolutionaries to worry about. One of them, after all, had murdered Plehve's predecessor, Sipiagin. Now Plehve was their target. Throughout 1903 and 1904, several attempts were made on his life. All failed, some because his agents had infiltrated the radical organizations planning to kill him and given warning.

One of the infiltrators was secret police agent Evno Azef. He had gone undercover to join the Socialist-Revolutionary Combat Organization (SR). After he had warned Plehve of one assassination plan and saved his life, Azef's loyalty began to be questioned by SR members. To save his own life, Azev himself arranged for the assassination of Plehve. This time there was no warning. On July 15, 1904, Plehve was blown to bits by a bomb thrown into his carriage.

The tsar had little time to mourn Plehve. His country was already fighting the Russo-Japanese War—and losing. On February 8, 1904, the Japanese fleet had staged a surprise nighttime torpedo assault on the Russian fleet at Port Arthur, the most heavily fortified naval base of the Imperial Russian Pacific fleet. Port Arthur was a strategically located deepwater harbor, and Russia's only ice-free port on the Pacific. However, it was not a part of mainland Russia. It was in China, situated on the southern tip of the Liao-tung Peninsula. Russia had leased Port Arthur from China in 1898.

Despite its internal problems, the tsarist government was committed to expanding its territory and its control over Pacific trade routes. Port Arthur gave Russia strategic control over Japanese sea-lanes. Also, part of the deal with the Chinese enabled Russia to build an extension of the Trans-Siberian Railroad through Manchuria, a province of China. This substantially cut the travel time to the Russian port of Vladivostok on the Sea of Japan. Russia had moved troops into Manchuria in violation of its agreement with China. Korea bordered on Manchuria, and lay between Vladivostok and Port Arthur like a ripe plum waiting to be plucked.

Korea was an independent nation. It had previously been occupied by both China and Japan, and was still considered to be in Japan's sphere of influence. It was a buffer between Russia and Japan. Russia's actions in Manchuria were a threat to Korea's independence. The Japanese justified the attack on Port Arthur as a preemptive strike against Russia before it could occupy Korea. The Korean government agreed and allowed Japan to use Korea as a base for operations against Russia.

THE RUSSIAN DEFEATS

The initial Japanese attack sank two Russian battleships and a cruiser, blocking the entrance to the Port Arthur harbor. Two other warships were trapped and disabled off the west coast of Korea. It was "a crippling blow to Russian military plans in Korea and Manchuria." The disabling of another Russian battleship and three Russian cruisers made it possible for "the Japanese to land troops . . . in Korea and Manchuria." Meanwhile, the rest of Russia's Pacific fleet was "ice-bound at Vladivostok."[15]

Three Russian infantry brigades and one artillery brigade invaded Korea from Manchuria. It was not a large enough force for the task. The bulk of the Russian army was in European Russia, and "it would take ten weeks to transport a sizable force by rail to the theater of war."[16] In March 1904 the Japanese bombarded Vladivostok and destroyed what was left of the Russian Pacific fleet. In April, following a battle between the two forces, the Russian army was in full retreat.

Having cut off the harbor, the Japanese laid siege to Port Arthur by land. The siege lasted for six months before the Russians surrendered. Half of the 45,000 Russian soldiers who defended the city were either killed or wounded. Heavy Russian casualties had by now become commonplace in the war and were adding to the unrest on the home front.

"BLOODY SUNDAY"

There were more than five hundred strikes and protests in the cities of Russia in 1904. Most had to do with labor unrest. At the end of the year, the tsar grudgingly agreed to reforms proposed by liberal nobles. However, little action was taken to implement the reforms. The tsar had flatly turned down the main demand. "I shall never, under any circumstances," he said, "agree to a representative form of government."[17] Democracy was out of the question.

On a Sunday morning in January 1905, more than 150,000 workers converged on the tsar's Winter Palace in St. Petersburg. Their leader was Father Gapon, a priest. He wanted to present "a Humble and Loyal Address to the Tsar begging him to improve the condition of the workers."[18]

The demonstrators carried icons and crosses and sang hymns. They were met by 12,000 troops. "The czar . . . ordered his troops to fire on the unarmed protestors." More than 500 marchers were killed. Many hundreds more were wounded. "Bloody Sunday," it was reported, "struck a death blow to the traditional affection the Russians feel for their czar, or 'Little Father,' and ended the workers' belief that the czar has been kept ignorant of their problems by his advisors." Three weeks later, Tsar Nicholas met with a committee of workers and announced that "I forgive them" for Bloody Sunday. This unfeeling response turned their anger to fury. Father Gapon was driven to outright sedition. "There is no Tsar!" he proclaimed.[19]

The radicals sent a more deadly message. In February, the tsar's uncle, Grand Duke Sergei Aleksandrovich, was killed by a bomb thrown in his lap as his carriage approached the Kremlin palace, a seat of government, in Moscow. As governor-general of Moscow, Grand Duke Aleksandrovich had established a reputation for incompetence and brutality. His wife, Grand Duchess Elizabeta Feodorovna, had acted on a warning not to ride in his carriage with him, and so was spared.

THE POTEMKIN MUTINY

Less than a month later, on March 13, the Russian army suffered a major defeat by the Japanese at Mukden in southern Manchuria. There were roughly 200,000 Russian casualties. There had already been antiwar demonstrations in St. Petersburg and the provinces. Now the unrest spread as landlords and government officials were attacked by mobs in rural villages across Russia.

The Mukden defeat was followed by more bad news. In May 1905, Russia's Baltic fleet sailed halfway around the world to confront the Japanese and suffered a major reverse, losing twelve warships. It was obvious to the most illiterate peasant that the war was lost, yet it dragged on, and the casualties mounted.

Russia, however, still had a fleet in the Black Sea, far from the war zone. Its most powerful battleship was the *Potemkin*, lying at anchor in the harbor at Odessa. On June 27, 1905, the crew aboard the *Potemkin* mutinied. The mutiny was set off by a mess officer murdering a sailor who complained that his soup was watery. The dead sailor's shipmates killed the officer and then went on to slay the captain and most of the other officers aboard the *Potemkin*. They threw the bodies into Odessa harbor. The red flag of revolution was raised over the ship, and the mutiny then spread to two other naval vessels in the harbor.

Meanwhile, a general strike had broken out in the city of Odessa. Troops were firing on rioting workers. A bomb was exploded in front of a cathedral. Fires raged along the waterfront. The Black Sea fleet was converging on the *Potemkin*, but the ship managed to slip away and surrender to Romanian authorities. Subsequently, eight *Potemkin* sailors were returned to Russia and put to death.

THE WAR ENDS

Following the *Potemkin* mutiny, unrest in Russia became too great for the tsar to ignore. To appease the people, in August he established the Duma, a Russian parliament. However, it had no real power. It could make recommendations to the tsar, but it could not pass legislation. It was structured so that its members represented the most conservative elements of Russian society.

In any case, the tsar had waited too long to act. Liberal, democratic, Socialist, and radical groups had formed a temporary alliance to organize general strikes in major cities. In Poland, Finland, the Baltic provinces, and the territory of Georgia, nationalist movements were fueling the rebellion. Army units along the Trans-Siberian Railroad rioted. Peasant uprisings were spreading throughout the provinces.

Cossacks fought the rebel peasants. They were aided by groups known as Black Hundreds, antirevolutionaries who sought out and killed those they considered agitators. Illogically, the Jews, who had suffered greatly from peasant pogroms, were now accused by the Black Hundreds of being behind the peasants' uprisings. On November 8, 1905, in Odessa, a pogrom instigated by Black Hundreds, army officers, and government officials resulted in the deaths of more than a thousand Jews.

By then the Russo-Japanese War had been over for two months. Japan had "achieved virtually all of its original war aims, including Russian withdrawal from Manchuria." Russia pledged "not to interfere with Japanese actions in Korea." Russia ceded Port Arthur to Japan. A peace treaty had been negotiated by President Theodore Roosevelt of the United States. It was signed on September 5, 1905, at Portsmouth, New Hampshire.[20]

On October 13, 1905, the first call for revolution by a soviet leader was raised. A soviet was a worker's council, a rough type of labor union. The leader who issued the call to arms was twenty-six-year-old Leon Trotsky. Following Trotsky's rallying cry, workers' soviets were organizing for revolution in cities throughout Russia.

Count Sergei Witte, the Russian prime minister, warned Tsar Nicholas that the country was on the verge of a revolution, which could "sweep away a thousand years of history."[21] The tsar's choices were either to abdicate (step down), appoint a military dictator, or introduce genuine reforms. On October 30, with his back to the wall, the tsar issued the October Manifesto. It promised a constitution and a democratically elected Duma.

The revolutionaries were not satisfied. The tsar had broken too many promises in the past to make these reforms believable. As long as he remained in power, tyranny would continue to rule. Still, some workers returned to their jobs. Some peasants laid down their arms and renewed their childlike faith in the tsar as a benign monarch. There was enough of a lull in the violence by December 16 for authorities to arrest the organizers of the soviets, including Leon Trotsky.

Immediately a new general strike was called in Moscow. "Barricades were erected and there was fighting in the streets." This time, however, strong radical leadership was lacking. Authorities were able to put down the uprising. Troops were sent to Poland, the Baltic provinces, and Georgia where "the suppression of the rebellions was particularly bloody." By the beginning of 1906, the government had regained control of the Trans-Siberian Railroad and of the army. The Russian Revolution of 1905 was over.[22]

CHAPTER
THREE

THE ARCHITECT OF
REVOLUTION

> **A specter is haunting Europe—
> the specter of Communism.**
>
> Opening words of **The Communist Manifesto**
> by Karl Marx and Friedrich Engels

The revolution of 1905 was the prelude to the Communist revolution of 1917. The person whose theories most influenced both revolutions, as well as the governments that ruled the Soviet Union throughout most of the twentieth century, was not Russian. He was a German who at various times lived in France, Belgium, and Great Britain. For eleven years he worked as the London correspondent for an American newspaper. His major works were researched and written in the reading room of the British Museum in London. They spelled out his ideas on the causes of oppression, poverty, and suffering, and detailed a plan for banishing them from the earth. His name was Karl Marx. His theories were called Marxism. His followers were called Marxists. Throughout its rise and fall, "all seven leaders" of the Soviet Union "considered themselves Marxists."[1]

YOUNG KARL MARX

By the time the Communists took over Russia, Karl Marx had been dead for more than thirty years. He had died of a lung abscess on March 14, 1883. He was born almost sixty-five years earlier on May 5, 1818, in Trier, Prussia (now Germany). His father was an attorney, a Jew who shortly before his son was born converted to Christianity for job security and probably to protect the child from the anti-Semitism prevalent at the time. Karl was the eldest of nine children. Not much is known about his mother or his siblings.

Karl Marx attended a Lutheran elementary school, and then a high school that was placed under government surveillance because it was suspected of spreading liberal teachings—theories of democracy, or socialism. He did well in all his subjects with the exception of history, the very subject that would play such an important part in his future writings. He was seventeen years old when he graduated, the youngest member of his class.

Following his graduation in 1835, Karl enrolled in the University of Bonn. Here he met Jenny von Westphalen. The daughter of a Socialist who tutored Marx, Jenny was smart, attractive, and four years older than Karl. They became secretly engaged. It would be seven years before they finally married. At least part of the delay had to do with Karl's irresponsibility. He was jailed for drunkenness, ran up bills he couldn't pay, and fought a duel. Finally his angry father had him transferred from Bonn to the University of Berlin where Karl finally settled down to study law and philosophy.

HEGEL'S DIALECTIC

In Berlin, as in most of the great cities of Europe and America at that time, there were all sorts of radical theories and reform movements focused on improving the lives of the poor and downtrodden. Much of this activity was inflamed by the ongoing industrial revolution—the development of power sources and factories, which were more efficient and profitable, and could produce more goods faster than the manual labor of the past. Over the previous century huge numbers of craft laborers, such as weavers, glassblowers, metalworkers, and smiths, had moved from the land to seek employment in the factories and mines. As those who had run the shops and provided the services also moved on to the industrial centers, whole communities vanished. Young people left the farms in search of a better life in the cities.

Over time, there was a mass movement from rural areas to urban centers. As a result, the cities became much more crowded. Housing became scarce and rents rose. Prices for goods in the cities were much higher than in the country. People used to foraging for food from the land in the worst of times now found that their wages in the coal mines of Wales, the sweat-shops of New York, or the linen mills of Belfast, were not enough to feed their families. They lived in slums where disease spread freely. These conditions, many radical thinkers felt, made society ripe for revolution. That view was commonly accepted among intellectuals at universities like the one Karl Marx attended in Berlin.

He joined a student party called the Doctor's Club.[2] It was "a hard-drinking, boisterous discussion group which met at a local café."[3] Members were called Young Hegelians because of their commitment to the ideas of Georg Wilhelm Friedrich Hegel.[4] The German philosopher's ideas, however, were very complicated and not easy to understand. On his deathbed in 1831, Hegel complained that "only one man ever understood me, and," he added, "he didn't understand me."[5]

Marx, however, understood Hegel's theory well enough to apply it in a way the philosopher had never anticipated. In Hegel's view, the world is made up of opposing forces, which create tension and conflict. The resolution of that tension and conflict is human progress. The process is called the dialectic. The dialectic was what Marx would adapt from Hegel.

During his university years, Marx "began moving rapidly toward atheism and also talked vaguely of political action."[6] By the time he graduated in 1841, Marx had already gained recognition as an up-and-coming theorist of radical principles. A Socialist leader, a friend of Marx at that time, said that "he combines with the deepest philosophical earnestness the most biting wit."[7]

MARRIAGE AND COMMUNISM

After graduation, Marx became a journalist. He wrote for the *Rheinische Zeitung*, a Cologne newspaper. Eventually becoming editor, he wrote articles condemning censorship and defending freedom of the press. He expressed "the view that there should be no private property."[8] Eventually, the Prussian government shut down the newspaper.

In June 1843, Marx and Jenny von Westphalen were finally married. They moved to Paris and started a family. A variety of Socialist movements

Karl Marx, about 1880

were flourishing in Paris. Marx became involved with leaders of the revolutionary workers' movements, and his views became more radical. He shifted left from radical democracy and socialism to communism.

Communism, "a term of ancient origin, originally meant a system of society in which property was owned by the community and all citizens shared in the enjoyment of the common wealth, more or less according to their need."[9] On a small scale, many idealistic Socialists had set up small Communist communities. For a variety of reasons, most of them had failed.

Marx, however, was beginning to view communism in larger terms. He was applying Hegel's dialectic to materialism—the theory that "men's mental and spiritual life, their ideas and aims, reflect their material conditions of existence."[10] In other words, one's economic status, living conditions, and property determine how one thinks about things. Dialectical materialism says that if people's economic situation is changed, their ideas will change. Marx, believing that only conflict brought progress, saw the industrial revolution as having created hardships, would bring about a reaction from the workers affected. He believed this reaction could be shaped into a revolution, which would result in universal ownership of property and a classless society.

Dialectical materialism would bring about the Russian Revolution and influence the policies of the Soviet Union for more than seventy years. Karl Marx had redefined the meaning of the word "communism." In the future, leaders Vladimir Lenin and Joseph Stalin would pollute its meaning with terror.

THE COMMUNIST MANIFESTO

In Paris, Marx met Friedrich Engels, and they reached "complete agreement on all theoretical matters."[11] Engels became Marx's lifelong collaborator, aiding him with research, editing, and rewriting, and helped to support him financially. He was able to do this because his father was a prosperous mill owner, and one day Friedrich Engels would become part owner of the business. Nevertheless, Engels was a dedicated Communist.

In 1845 the French government responded to Marx's pamphlets and writings in left-wing publications, urging the working class to rise up, by expelling him from the country. Engels accompanied Marx to Belgium and later to London. Here, Marx and Engels worked on *The Communist Manifesto*. It was published in London as a pamphlet in January 1848.

The *Manifesto* proclaimed that all history "is the history of class struggle," the conflict between "oppressor and oppressed." It declared that world society was "splitting up into two great hostile camps . . . bourgeoisie and proletariat." It defined bourgeoisie as "owners of the means of . . . production and employers of wage labour." The proletariat were "wage labourers who, having no means of production of their own, are reduced to selling their labour power in order to live." The middle class—small shop owners, farmers, tradespeople, anyone who did not work on salary—were considered bourgeois, and not dependable as revolutionaries.[12]

Working people "have no country," according to the pamphlet, and so would not fight against each other in a war.[13] Among the *Manifesto*'s demands were an end to private property and inherited wealth; nationalization of banks, communications networks, transportation facilities, factories, and farmland; free public schools; abolition of child labor; and laws requiring all people to work. After remarking that "the proletarians have nothing to lose but their chains," the *Manifesto* ends with a capitalized call to arms: "WORKING MEN OF ALL COUNTRIES, UNITE!"[14]

TROUBLES AND TRAGEDY

Coincidentally, within weeks of the publication of the *Manifesto,* revolution broke out in France, Italy, and Austria. Marx returned to Germany just as things were heating up there as well. Here he did an about-face, urging that *The Communist Manifesto* be shelved so that German workers could join with the middle class to overthrow the government. He published a newspaper advocating that Germany establish a constitutional democracy and declare war on Russia, which was supporting a Prussian monarchy as a bulwark against the Communist revolution in France. When the king of Prussia put down the rebellion, Marx was brought to trial on several charges, including urging nonpayment of taxes. Although he was undoubtedly guilty, the jury acquitted him. When he resumed publishing his revolutionary newspaper, Marx was once again deported from

Germany. The final issue of his newspaper was printed in red, which symbolized both blood and revolution. It "caused a great sensation."[15]

Marx returned to London in August 1849. He spent the rest of his life there. It was an extremely hard life. For eleven years, his only steady source of income was as correspondent for the *New York Daily Tribune*. He wrote some five hundred articles and editorials for the *Tribune*, but at two pounds sterling (approximately ten dollars) per piece, it wasn't enough to keep him and his family from living in poverty. In April 1850 the Marx family was evicted from their home, and their furniture was confiscated. In November, one-year-old Guido Marx died.

Troubles and tragedies came one after another. In June 1851, Frederick, a son fathered by Marx, was born out of wedlock to a housekeeper. Marx was sued for nonpayment of bills. Nor had he money for rent, taxes, or payment of debts. His children had no shoes, and the family had no coal for heat. Marx pawned his coat, and his wife, Jenny, pawned her clothes to pay the landlord so they wouldn't be evicted again. In 1852 their new baby, Franziska, died. Two years later eight-year-old Edgar Marx died. Jenny delivered a stillborn child, and then came down with smallpox.

Karl Marx was writing about poverty under capitalism, and he was living the horrors he was writing about. Every day he went to the British Museum and worked on his major work, *Das Kapital*. He suffered from rheumatism, bronchitis, lung abscesses, gallbladder attacks, and a host of minor ailments, but he kept on writing.

DAS KAPITAL

Despite his ailments, Marx also stayed active in European revolutionary politics. He was influential in organizing and unifying the International Working Men's Association, which became known as the First International. By 1869 its membership had grown to 800,000. Around this time, Marx came into conflict with Mikhail Bakunin, the leading European anarchist of the period. Bakunin believed that "the passion for destruction is also a creative passion."[16] Bakunin, who was Russian, believed that world revolution would begin with "the Russian peasantry, with its propensity for violence and its uncurbed revolutionary instincts."[17] Marx, who did "not trust any Russian," was convinced that revolution had to take place in an industrialized country, which Russia was not, and could only be brought about by workers seizing control of the means of production.[18] By 1872 the quarrel led to a breakup of the First International. The membership fragmented into many parties, which found it difficult to work together.

Marx nevertheless continued to work in the radical movement and to write his three-volume study of capitalism, *Das Kapital*. The first volume was published in Berlin in 1867. A Russian translation was reviewed by the tsar's censors in March 1872. "It is possible to state with certainty," they concluded, "that very few people in Russia will read it, and even fewer will understand it."[19] They decided not to prevent its publication.

The censors were mistaken. The first print run of *Das Kapital*, three thousand copies, sold out within a year. Large sales continued with additional printings. It became "must" reading for Russian intellectuals and dissident university students. Marx, who continued to believe that revolution would not occur in preindustrialized Russia, had to admit that in Russia *Das Kapital* was "read and valued more than anywhere." Royalties earned by *Das Kapital* eased the author's financial difficulties, as did an increase in the money he received from Engels, who had recently inherited some of his father's mills. Nevertheless, Marx began suffering bouts of depression. These grew worse with the death of his wife, Jenny, in 1881. Two years later Karl Marx himself died.

More family tragedy followed his death. In 1898, Marx's daughter Eleanor committed suicide. In 1911 his daughter Laura and her husband also killed themselves. Only Frederick Marx, the son born out of wedlock, was still alive when the Russian Revolution exploded. He alone, of all Karl Marx's children, observed that despite his father's belief to the contrary, *Das Kapital* had indeed "led to revolution" in Russia.[20]

CHAPTER FOUR

INTRIGUE AND MURDER

The Marxists who would one day rule Russia held their First Party Congress in Minsk in 1898. They called themselves the "Russian Social Democratic Labour Party."[1] Nine Socialists attended the secret meeting. They set Marxist goals for the party and then adjourned. As they left, they were arrested by the police.

THE PARTY SPLIT

Mindful of the risks, the Second Party Congress wasn't held in Russia, but in Brussels, Belgium, in 1903. Vladimir Lenin dominated the meeting. He and his followers insisted that "party membership be restricted to professional revolutionaries." Calling themselves "Bolsheviks" (those of the majority), they won control of the party's central committee. They dubbed their opponents, who did not agree with the membership restrictions, "Mensheviks" (those of the minority).[2]

Although both Bolsheviks and Mensheviks were Marxists, they disagreed on how to interpret Marx. Both accepted that Russia must become a capitalist nation before a Socialist revolution could succeed. However, "the Mensheviks believed that, in view of Russia's economic backwardness, it would take a long time before such a revolution could take place, and that the immediate task was to work for a middle-class liberal revolution," which would "get rid of the autocratic tsarist regime." This meant working with non-Marxist liberal parties. Lenin and the Bolsheviks thought that cooperating with non-Marxists would lead to compromises that would destroy the goal of world revolution. They believed in "full-time revolutionaries" who would "direct the workers' understanding of their true class interest." To Mensheviks, this was "an anti-Marxist heresy," which gave power to an elite few, rather than to the workers.[3]

The rift between Bolsheviks and Mensheviks had widened by 1906 when elections to Russia's first Duma (parliament) were held. Lenin controlled the Bolsheviks with an iron fist while alienating the Mensheviks by calling them "traitors to the Marxist cause."[4] Nevertheless, the two factions continued to exist side by side in the Russian Social Democratic Labour party.

THE FIRST DUMA

On Lenin's orders, elections to the first Duma were boycotted by the Bolsheviks. Local branches of the Mensheviks were free to participate or not, as they saw fit. Most did not. The Duma was elected by a system weighted in favor of the wealthy and the peasantry, whom the tsar considered conservative. He was wrong. The peasant representatives in the first Duma often sided with a coalition of liberal groups demanding extensive reforms. These were led by the Constitutional Democrats, more familiarly known as Kadets.

The demands—"redistribution of landowners' estates to peasants with or without compensation, amnesty for political prisoners, equal rights for Jews and for religious dissenters, autonomy for Poland"—were unacceptable to the government.[5] The "government" was the tsar and the upper house State Council appointed by him to "serve as a brake on the Duma."[6] All of the Duma's attempts to pass reforms resulted in a stalemate. Finally, the tsar dissolved the Duma on July 8, 1906. It had lasted exactly seventy-two days.

During that time, the Socialist Revolutionary party had launched a new terrorist campaign. Like the Bolsheviks, and most Mensheviks, the

Socialist Revolutionaries had boycotted the Duma. They were following the policies of the long-dead anarchist Mikhail Bakunin, who had advocated assassination as a weapon to bring down the government. In 1906 and 1907, Socialist Revolutionaries and other left-wing terrorists killed more than nine thousand people in Russia.

For the most part, Bolsheviks were not involved in these killings. They were, however, carrying out a series of robberies to obtain the funds needed to finance their political operations. The Mensheviks condemned such criminal activity. The split between Bolsheviks and Mensheviks grew.

PRIME MINISTER STOLYPIN

The murders and robberies infuriated Tsar Nicholas. Orders were issued to crack down on all groups opposed to the imperial regime. What followed, according to Prime Minister Sergei Witte, was "a brutal and excessive, and often totally unjustified, series of repressive measures." Between 1906 and 1909, more than 5,000 politicals were sentenced to death. An additional 38,000 were jailed, or sent to labor camps in Siberia. Cossacks, drunk on vodka, hung innocent peasants from the trees, raped their wives and daughters, and committed other terrible atrocities. In the Russian Baltics, a six-month campaign of terror by army units destroyed tens of thousands of buildings. Baltic peasants and workers were flogged. Twelve hundred people were executed. The tsar was pleased. He praised the commanding officer of the Baltic operation for "acting splendidly."[7]

During this period, Count Witte was replaced by Petr Arkadevich Stolypin as prime minister. The tsar wanted a "strong man" to deal with the unrest, and he believed that Stolypin's "country gentleman's knowledge of how to dominate peasants" made him ideal for the job. He was not disappointed. Stolypin would long be remembered for his merciless campaign against the tsar's enemies. Railway cars used to carry exiles to Siberia were called "Stolypin carriages." Hangmen's nooses were dubbed "Stolypin's neckties."[8]

Despite his brutality, Prime Minister Stolypin recognized that reforms must take place in Russia. He used his power to institute such reforms, but he always acted as a royalist. The reforms had to be handed down from the tsar, not rise up from the people being provoked by Socialist agitators. The people must bring their grievances to the tsar through his appointed representatives. To set an example for this, Stolypin held open house every Sunday for those seeking help or favors from the tsar's prime minister.

On the afternoon of Sunday, August 12, 1906, the foyer to the Stolypin villa was crowded with supplicants. Three terrorists, two of them dressed as police officers, came to the door and asked to be allowed to join those in the foyer. A suspicious guard stopped them, but it was too late. They threw briefcases loaded with explosives into the villa. Along with the terrorists themselves, twenty-seven petitioners and guards were killed. Two of Stolypin's children were injured, but Stolypin himself was not hurt. It was only the first of many such attempts on his life.

THE TSAR'S "CONSCIENCE"

In August 1906, Stolypin prevailed upon the tsar to respond to a major complaint of the peasants. The patches of land they had been able to buy following the Emancipation Proclamation of 1861 were too small or too nonproductive to support them and their families. They were farmers, and they desperately needed more land to plant their crops. Thanks to Stolypin, the tsar agreed to sell them land belonging to the Romanov family, as well as state land. Easy credit was extended and mortgages were arranged. As a result, between 1906 and 1916, three million peasants moved to arable land in western Siberia and the plains of Central Asia.

Another of Stolypin's attempts at reform was less successful. This was his effort to do away with many of the restrictions on Jews. This policy had encouraged savage pogroms. These brought repeated protests from the United States where, at that time, anti-Semitism existed, but violence against Jews was not condoned. The brutality of the tsar's anti-Semitic programs had poisoned relations between the two countries. Also, French and other foreign financial institutions were withholding loans from Russia because they thought government-sponsored pogroms made the tsarist regime unstable.

The Imperial Russian Council of Ministers voted in favor of Stolypin's proposal to do away with anti-Semitic laws. Rasputin, who by this time was wielding considerable influence on the tsar through Tsarina Alexandra, also championed equal rights for Jews. Tsar Nicholas, however, flatly rejected Stolypin's measure. His reason? "Conscience," he said.[9] The United States rejected that reason in 1911 when, acting on a recommendation by President William Howard Taft, the Senate renounced the U. S.-Russian Treaty of 1832 because of official anti-Semitism in Russia.

THE SECOND DUMA

One of Stolypin's early problems was the convening of the second Duma on February 20, 1907. Both the Social Democrats and the Socialist Revolutionaries had abandoned their boycotts and were now represented in the second Duma. Socialist parties outnumbered right-wing parties by two to one. This did not include the middle-of-the-road Kadets, whose goal was reform through a constitutional monarchy like Great Britain's, a system that would leave the tsar in place while placing the reins of government in the hands of a democratically elected parliament. Stolypin opposed this as he did all measures that threatened the tsar's position as absolute monarch.

His main concern was not the Kadets, however, but the Socialist parties. The Socialist Revolutionaries had resolved to use the Duma to organize the masses for revolution. The Social Democrats, controlled by Lenin's Bolshevik faction, were determined to exploit conflicts between parties in the Duma, as well as clashes between the Duma and the tsar's government, to inflame the revolutionary movement while building support for their leadership. The leftist parties, in other words, wanted to sabotage the Duma so that the Russian people would reject it as useless and turn to revolution to relieve their hardships.

The second Duma drew up demands for reforms even more radical than those presented by the first Duma. They knew they would be rejected. It was a way of provoking the tsar into repressive actions that would increase the pressure for revolution. Eventually, the tactic pushed the tsar and Stolypin into dissolving the second Duma in June 1907, four months after it had held its first meeting.

Stolypin then changed the law for electing deputies to a new Duma. The right to vote was extended freely to the upper classes, but certain restrictions were imposed on the peasants and workers. Minority nationalities in Russia—Poles, Finns, Jews, and others— did not have the same voting rights as ethnic Russians. As a result, the third and fourth Dumas that followed were much more conservative than the first two.

REFORMS, RESTRICTIONS, AND RESERVATIONS

To some extent, over the next four years, Stolypin was able to succeed in his twin goals of maintaining the absolute power of the tsarist regime while pushing through reforms designed to ease resentment against it. Under Stolypin, political parties could meet openly, a free press sprang up, workers formed trade unions, money was made available to local governments for social services, and there were improvements in primary education. In particular, he continued his efforts on behalf of the peasants. His policy was "to put money, effort, and education into agriculture" so that "the countryside could no longer be milked for the benefit of other parts of the economy."[10] Stolypin wanted to turn the Russian peasant into a farmer-landowner-businessman, and to a remarkable extent he succeeded. It would be a decade and more before bolshevism and famine undid his work.

There were, however, many weak spots in Stolypin's reforms. For example, it was against the law for trade unions to strike. Local government officials throughout Russia were appointed by Stolypin to stop unrest before it got out of hand, but they were often corrupt and brutal, and frequently defied the laws backing up Stolypin's reforms. Finally, Stolypin cracked down on the universities, which were traditional centers of dissent. Students and professors reacted to stepped-up repression with mass protests. The intellectuals so despised by the tsar became even firmer opponents of the regime.

The intellectuals did not appreciate Stolypin's reforms, even though they would not have been allowed by the tsar under any other prime minister. Stolypin's influence over Nicholas was greater than anyone's except the tsarina. The tsar's decisions were often her decisions, but Alexandra's judgment was subject to the will of Rasputin. When Stolypin challenged that will, he reached the absolute limit of his influence over Tsar Nicholas.

RASPUTIN: EGO AND INFLUENCE

Stolypin brought to the tsar a secret police report on Rasputin's government intrigues, outlandish sexual behavior, and outright crimes. The tsar cut him short. "I know, Petr Arkadevich, that you are sincerely devoted to me. Perhaps everything you say is true. But I ask you never again to speak to me about Rasputin." On another occasion, when even more damaging evidence was presented to him by the president of the Duma, Nicholas protested that Rasputin "can relieve the sufferings of my son by a strange power. The tsarina's reliance upon him is a matter for the family, and I will allow no one to meddle in my affairs."[11]

Of course, Rasputin's activities were having an effect well beyond the royal family. Because of his close relationship with them, he had great influence in government circles. Nobles seeking positions in the administration sought him out. Rasputin would make a recommendation to the tsarina, who would pass it on to the tsar. Soon a growing number of men in administrative positions and other high places were in his debt.

It became known that Rasputin accepted bribes. These might be in the form of money, jewels, or sexual favors. Ordinary people lined up outside his home every day to ask help in getting an apartment, to request letters of introduction for jobs as clerks, for auditions at theaters, or to beg for help in keeping their sons out of the army. Rasputin could help the little people because the important people he had helped owed him favors.

"I can do anything," he said frequently, and because he could get results so often, he was believed.[12] It followed that since he was believed, people high and low were eager to please him. He might not be the pipeline to the tsar in all cases, they reasoned, but then again, it might be dangerous to cross him. His confidence grew with each success, and with it, his ego— and his power.

THE DEATH OF STOLYPIN

Rasputin's alleged occult powers also inspired fear. There could be no doubt that he continued to bring the Tsarevich Alexis's bleeding under control. There were other successful healings, and as word of them spread,

Rasputin's reputation grew. Most of it was due to his hypnotic abilities, but these were not always used in medical situations. He also used hypnotism in his ongoing erotic pursuits. There were rumors that he hypnotized the tsarina.

Stolypin was fearful that the relationship between Rasputin and the tsarina might compromise the tsarist regime. The tsarina did not like Stolypin and had managed through her influence on the tsar to block many of his reforms. She had also managed to have General Pavel Grigorevich Kurlov appointed chief of the secret police over Stolypin's protests. Kurlov had Stolypin watched, and reported back to the tsarina. In this way she learned that Stolypin had Rasputin under surveillance. The tsarina grew fearful of Stolypin's intentions toward Rasputin. It was a spy-counterspy situation, even more tangled than most of the intrigues so typical of Imperial Russia.

The situation came to a head on September 1, 1911. Stolypin had attended a performance at the Kiev Municipal Theater. Tsar Nicholas and his daughters sat in a box not far from him as he chatted with some friends during an intermission. Suddenly a young man pulled a pistol from behind his theater program and fired twice, hitting the prime minister in the hand and chest.

Following the shooting, "rumours immediately began to circulate that Kurlov had commissioned the murder."[13] Some said he was acting for the United Nobility, a right-wing organization pledged to defend aristocrats' property rights against Stolypin's reforms. Others whispered that Kurlov was acting for the tsarina.

Stolypin did not die immediately after being shot. He was rushed to a hospital, and it was predicted that he would recover. However, his wounds became infected, and on the evening of September 5, 1911, he passed away.

He left behind the legend of his initial reaction to the shooting. That night in the Kiev Municipal Theater, with the royal family looking on as blood stained his tunic, Stolypin had seated himself, and then looked up from the wound. "I am happy," he said in a loud, firm voice, "to die for the Tsar."[14]

CHAPTER FIVE

THE BOLSHEVIK LEADERS

> ## You cannot make a revolution with silk gloves.
>
> Premier Joseph Stalin of Russia

During 1911, tensions within the Russian Social Democratic Labour party were coming to a head. In Switzerland, far from Russia, "Lenin's dictatorial methods and his complete lack of scruples alienated some of his staunchest supporters."[1] Even some loyal Bolsheviks had grown weary of the ongoing intrigues and squabbles. In the upper party ranks, the differences between the Bolsheviks and Mensheviks could not be resolved.

THE FINAL BREAK

Lenin had set up a Bolshevik treasury independent of the Social Democratic Labour party treasury. It was funded by donations from patrons, some quite wealthy, dues from Bolshevik party members, and—primarily—from robberies of post offices, banks, trains, and railroad stations. There was also a Bolshevik counterfeiting operation cashing phony currency in foreign countries. Lenin's control of the Bolshevik wealth made him the most powerful person in the party.

His control over the money also made him a target of the Mensheviks. They lamented that the party image, because of Lenin, was that of a gang of thieves rather than a Socialist workers' movement. They accused him of personally mishandling the money and of outright theft. But Lenin had the power, and he knew it. He called a party conference for January 1912 in Prague.

The Prague Conference was the final break between Bolsheviks and Mensheviks. They never again held a joint meeting under the Russian Social Democratic Labour party banner. The core members of the two groups were permanently alienated. Nevertheless, in Russia rank-and-file Bolsheviks and Mensheviks continued to work together. Indeed, during the fourth Duma, "the seven Menshevik and six Bolshevik deputies acted in a more cooperative spirit" than Lenin desired.[2]

TROTSKY: THE EARLY YEARS

Leon Trotsky, who had been "Lenin's most implacable opponent on the question of the organization of the party" at the 1903 party congress, organized a conference of all Social Democrats to meet in Vienna in August 1912.[3] His purpose was to mend the breach between Bolsheviks and Mensheviks. Despite his opposition to Lenin, Trotsky had not joined the Mensheviks. It was a bitter disappointment for Trotsky when Lenin refused to attend.

Five years would pass before Trotsky and Lenin patched up their differences and worked together to seize control of the revolution, which would sweep over Russia. Along with Joseph Stalin and Grigori Zinoviev, Trotsky would be a key figure in the implementation of Lenin's hard-line policies. He would never question morality, or balk at brutality, if it was for the good of the revolution. The revolution always came first with Trotsky.

Trotsky had been born Lev Davidovich Bronstein in 1879 in Yanovka, Ukraine. His family was Jewish, and at the age of seven he had been sent to a religious school. He was unhappy there, and after being tutored at home for a year, he entered St. Paul's Realschule in Odessa. After seven years, he moved on to the seaport city of Nikolaev to complete his schooling. Here Trotsky joined a left-wing discussion group sponsored by the People's Will.

Aleksandra Sokolovskaya, a dedicated Marxist, was also a member. She was drawn to Trotsky, as were other members of the group, by his

Leon Trotsky,
in a photo taken in 1922

sharp intellect and ability as an orator. He would argue Marxism with her, but in the end he was drawn to it. He became involved with the South Russian Workers' Union and took part in its underground actions. When the group was infiltrated by police spies, Trotsky was arrested, tried for revolutionary activities, convicted, and exiled to Siberia for four years. Aleksandra Sokolovskaya went to Siberia with Trotsky, and they were married there.

"PERMANENT REVOLUTION"

In Siberia, Aleksandra gave birth to two daughters. She urged Trotsky to escape, but when he managed to follow her advice, Aleksandra remained behind. It was to be a permanent separation and the end of their marriage. Using a false passport with the name "Leon Trotsky" on it, after crossing many borders, he made his way to London. Here, keeping the name, Trotsky joined Lenin, and worked on a small left-wing newspaper that Lenin was putting out. As time passed, friction built up between them, and it finally exploded during the 1903 party Congress. After his break with Lenin, Trotsky moved to Paris where he met and married Natalya Sedova, by whom he would have two sons.

When revolution broke out in 1905, Trotsky hurried back to Russia. Arrested for his participation, he was sentenced to a life term in Siberia. Here he wrote *Results and Prospects*, which would have a major influence in left-wing circles. In it he spelled out his theory of "permanent revolution." To explain it, Trotsky applied Marxist theory to real-life conditions in Russia—"a backward country in revolutionary ferment"— and said that the ongoing turmoil would eventually "create a permanent state of revolution internationally as well." This was important because it would later become Communist Russia's policy of exporting revolution throughout the world.[4]

After his book was finished, Trotsky once again escaped from Siberia. He settled in Vienna and supported himself as a journalist. He became the editor of a Viennese paper called *Pravda*, which would later become the state-run newspaper of the Communist Russian government. From 1912 to 1913, Trotsky was a foreign correspondent in the small-scale Balkan Wars, which preceded World War I.

ZINOVIEV: THE LOYAL DISCIPLE

Trotsky was destined to be one of the three major colleagues of Lenin, who would raise him to power on the crest of revolution. The other two were Grigori Evseevich Zinoviev and Joseph Stalin. Unlike Trotsky, their support of Lenin had not wavered during the years leading up to the Russian Revolution.

Zinoviev, like Trotsky, was Jewish. He was born in 1883 in the southern Russian town of Ylizavetgrad. He had a middle-class upbringing, and a fairly good education. When he was only seventeen years old he became involved with the Russian Social Democratic Labour party. By the time he was twenty, Zinoviev had become a devoted disciple of Lenin. He remained loyal to Lenin when the party split into opposing factions, and he became a dedicated Bolshevik. Like Trotsky, he participated in the 1905 revolution. Unlike Trotsky, he escaped the country without being caught.[5]

On July 26, 1914, two days before World War I began, Lenin and Zinoviev—who was now widely regarded as Lenin's second in command—were in Vienna. Considered enemy aliens by the Austrian authorities, they were arrested as suspected spies. They spent ten days in jail before Lenin was identified as "an enemy of tsarism," and they were released.[6] Lenin left Vienna for Switzerland in an Austrian military mail train, a sign that the government regarded him as a possible asset in the war that was starting against Russia. Zinoviev joined Lenin in Switzerland two weeks later.

STALIN: "MAN OF STEEL"

When World War I broke out, the third of Lenin's major comrades, Joseph Stalin, was living in exile in a remote penal settlement in the Yenisei-Turukhansk region of northern Siberia. In the winter the temperature fell to forty degrees below zero Centigrade, and the winters were nine months long. He lived in virtual isolation, ice fishing for food, smoking the pipe that would become his trademark, and reading old books. He had no access to newspapers. It was a six-week journey by sled to the Trans-Siberian Railroad, but he had no sled. Throughout most of the war, Joseph Stalin was cut off from the world.

He bore his exile patiently. Hardship had always been his lot. Before he changed his name to Stalin, which means "man of steel,"[7] his passport had identified him as "Josif Djugashvili, peasant from the Gori District of Tiflis Province."[8] He had been born a peasant and was proud of it. In Stalin's view, peasants knew how to suffer—and how to make others suffer.

Stalin had been born in a two-room hut in Gori on December 21, 1879. His parents had four children, but he was the only one to survive. When he was five years old, he, too, almost died of smallpox. The disease left his face with deep pockmarks.

His father was a cobbler who regularly beat his wife and young son. When Stalin was eleven years old, shortly after his parents separated, his father was killed in a barroom brawl. Four years later Stalin entered a seminary in Tiflis. Here he "displayed a phenomenal talent for memorizing religious texts, as well as a deep interest in the Old and New Testaments."[9] At the same time, he became interested in the idea of revolution as a way of relieving the hardships of peasant life. His deepening involvement in revolutionary activities led to his being expelled from the seminary in 1899. Two years later he joined the Tiflis branch of the Russian Social Democratic Labour party and became involved in a May Day demonstration in which police opened fire on workers, killing fifteen of them. The following year he was arrested as a revolutionist for the first time. In 1903, at the age of twenty-four, Stalin was exiled to East Siberia.

KOBA: THE BANK ROBBER

During his first stay in Siberia, Stalin had more contact with other exiles than during his later times there. "I hung around mostly with criminals," he would later tell Nikita Khrushchev, the man who would succeed Stalin as leader of the Soviet Union.[10] After he escaped from exile in 1904 and went back to Tiflis, Stalin would put to use the skills he had picked up from these criminals.

Upon his return, Stalin sided with the Bolshevik faction of the Social Democrats. By now he was using the name Koba, and would continue to do so until he took the name Stalin. It was the name of the main character in *The Patricide*, a popular novel by Alexander Kazbegi. In the book, Koba is a Robin Hood-type hero "who defies the Cossacks, defends the rights of the peasants, and avenges his friends."[11] Soon Stalin was earning the name by "organizing bank robberies—the so-called 'expropriations'—in Georgia on behalf of Lenin and his secret Bolshevik Centre."[12]

In 1905, Stalin met Lenin for the first time at a Bolshevik conference in Finland. Later he met Zinoviev and Trotsky. They did not hit it off. Stalin distrusted intellectuals and disliked Jews. Unfairly and inaccurately, he grouped them with the Mensheviks as "circumcised Yids" and "cowards and peddlers." Trotsky shrugged off Stalin as "a gray and colorless mediocrity." Many years later, Stalin would order the deaths of both Zinoviev and Trotsky.[13]

Lenin, however, was quite impressed with Stalin. Here was a true proletariat in the Marxist sense, a revolutionary wage laborer who didn't hesitate to resort to crime for the good of the Bolshevik cause. An intellectual himself, Lenin had contempt for many of the intellectuals around him. But for Koba, the daring bank robber who acted while others talked and endlessly debated, Lenin had great admiration.

ANARCHISM OR SOCIALISM?

Stalin married Ekaterina Svanidze in June 1906. The following year, Ekaterina gave birth to a son, Yakov. Six months later she fell victim to typhus and died. From all reports, Stalin was heartbroken. Nevertheless, during that time he wrote a series of articles, *Anarchism or Socialism?*, which attracted wide attention in left-wing circles. Along with his activities as a bank robber, these pieces aroused the enmity of the Mensheviks.

Things came to a head when the Tiflis State Bank was robbed. The Mensheviks accused Stalin of being involved, and when he wasn't arrested, they accused him of being a police spy, and demanded that he be thrown out of the Social Democratic Labour party. Stalin was not expelled, but he did move from Tiflis to the Baku oil fields where he worked as a labor organizer. At that time, Baku was the most productive oil center in the world.

That fact didn't mean then what it does today. There were no cars or airplanes in Russia to run on gasoline refined from oil. Russia's substan-

Joseph Stalin in 1906

dard railway system ran on coal, and most transportation was by horse and wagon. Homes were heated by burning wood or coal. Since most of the world was not yet lit by electricity, the oil produced in Baku was for lighting lamps. It was sold around the world for that purpose, and it was central to the expansion of Russian trade.

THE PEASANTS' DREAM

The workers in the oil fields and the stations powering the pumps and derricks were Turks, Persians, Tatars, and Armenians, as well as Georgian peasants. The more skilled workers were Russians who had been banished to the oil fields because of their involvement in labor strife in some of the new factories that were starting up in Imperial Russia. They formed the nucleus for the soviets that Stalin began to organize. He was particularly effective in persuading the peasant laborers to join these soviets.

Stalin understood peasants in a way that Lenin and the other leftist leaders could not. Lenin's ultimate aim was to nationalize the farmland and have it run by a central government. Stalin understood that "even in their dreams, the peasants see the landlords' fields as their own property."[14] Lenin was sharply critical of Stalin's view. However, he would later reverse himself in order to get peasant backing for the revolution. Stalin's understanding of the peasants' position would prove to be important to the success of the revolution.

"Two years of revolutionary work among the oil workers of Baku hardened me as a practical fighter," Stalin wrote during one of his frequent terms in prison.[15] It also established him as a major Bolshevik figure. He became a member of the four-man bureau set up to organize Bolshevik activities inside Russia. He was in charge of publishing the first Russian underground issue of *Pravda*. He spent a month in Vienna in 1913 to study how Austrian Socialists had dealt with the conflicts among the different nationalities in the Austrian Empire. A week after returning to St. Petersburg, Stalin was arrested and shipped off to the farthest northern reaches of Siberia. Here he remained, cutting holes in the ice for his fishing line as World War I swept over Europe.

CHAPTER SIX

MOTHER RUSSIA'S DYING SONS

> ## A war between Austria and Russia would be a most useful thing for the revolution . . .
>
> Lenin in a 1913 letter to Maxim Gorky

A Marxist principle, to which all members of the international Socialist movement gave lip service, was that the workers of one country should not spill the blood of the workers of another country in a war. Such wars, Marx had reasoned, were fought over spoils, which profited only the ruling class on the winning side. However, as early as 1907 at the Stuttgart Congress of the Socialist International, various national delegations were proclaiming their patriotism as a higher duty than the betterment of the working class. Typical was the statement by a member of the German delegation. "It is not true that workers have no Fatherland," the speaker declared. "The love of humanity does not prevent us from being good Germans."[1]

Lenin, who was present, expressed horror at this betrayal of Marxism. He responded with a resolution, which the congress adopted. It pledged the working classes of all nations and their representatives to work to prevent the outbreak of war. However, if war broke out, while working to end it, they were to "exploit the crisis with all their strength to hasten the abolition of capitalism."[2] By 1914, when war did start, Lenin was committed to transforming it into revolution.

THE SCHLIEFFEN PLAN

World War I was inevitable. The saber rattling of Kaiser Wilhelm of Germany, who made no secret of his schemes for military conquest, had put Great Britain, France, and Russia on alert for at least seven years preceding the outbreak of war. The kaiser had always been considered the bad boy of the interrelated royal families of Europe. As a youth, when visiting his grandmother Queen Victoria of England, he had sometimes bullied his younger British cousins. As the adult ruler of Germany, Wilhelm had proclaimed that "there is no balance of power in Europe but me—me and my twenty-five army corps." He had told the young recruits in those army corps that "if your Emperor commands you to do so you must fire on your father and mother."[3]

Wilhelm's advisers "regarded the breakup of Russia and control of her resources as essential" to Germany's growth.[4] This would upset the balance of power in Europe, and France and Britain would react. Anticipating this, the head of the German general staff, Alfred von Schlieffen, had devised a plan by which German armies would crush France before Great Britain could come to its aid, and before Russian armies could effectively mobilize. The Schlieffen Plan called for the massive German Army to then swing east from conquered France and invade Russia, crushing the badly organized forces in its way.

The Russians were aware of the threat. The army was being reorganized. The roads and railways needed to move troops were being improved. However, the threat of war had been hanging over their heads for so long that the Imperial Russian government tended to put it on the back burner. Mounting turmoil inside Russia too often distracted the tsar and his advisers from the German menace.

It was taken more seriously in Britain. Wilhelm's British cousin George had been crowned king of England in 1910, and for the first four years of his reign the threat of German aggression had been his main foreign-policy concern. King George was an extremely popular monarch and, strangely enough, some of that popularity had rubbed off on Tsar Nicholas of Russia. He had "close blood ties with the British royal family. The obvious facial resemblance to his cousin King George V appealed . . . to popular sentiment in Britain."[5]

IGNITING THE POWDER KEG

On the eve of war, certain official and unofficial alliances were in place. Germany was aligned with the Austro-Hungarian Empire and the Ottoman Empire (Turkey). Britain was pledged to defend France and also Belgium. Russia was loosely allied with France and Britain, and had vowed to protect Serbia against aggression by Austria-Hungary.

Serbia was the powder keg, and the fuse was lit on June 28, 1914, in the city of Sarajevo, in Bosnia-Herzegovina. Archduke Francis Ferdinand of Austria, next in line to the throne of Emperor Francis Joseph I of Austria-Hungary, was visiting the city on a tour of military inspection with his wife, Sophie, the duchess of Hohenberg. They were riding in an open carriage when Serbian nationalist Gavrilo Princip emerged from the crowd lining the boulevard and shot them both dead.

Austria-Hungary reacted by making a series of demands on Serbia. When Serbia balked at them, Austria-Hungary threatened war. The threat was backed up by assurances from Kaiser Wilhelm that Germany would support the Austro-Hungarian Empire. The diplomatic jockeying came to a head on July 24, when Russia protested that "Austria-Hungary must not be allowed to crush Serbia."[6] Four days later Austria-Hungary declared war on Serbia.

On July 30, Russia ordered a general mobilization of its armies. The next day Germany sent the tsar an ultimatum threatening war if Russia didn't stop the mobilization within twenty-four hours. When Russia refused, on August 1, Germany declared war on Russia. Germany followed this up with an invasion of Belgium. This was in reality a massive troop movement toward France, and war was declared on France. On August 5, Austria-Hungary declared war on Russia.

World War I had begun. On September 5, 1914, Russia, France, and Great Britain signed the Treaty of London by which each country pledged not to make a separate peace with the Central Powers, as their foes' alliance was known. It was a pledge that would play an important part in the Russian Revolution. Meanwhile, in neutral Switzerland, where Lenin was making plans for the revolution, the family ties of the rulers of the battling nations had led to the conflict's being dubbed "The Cousins' War."

ALEKSANDR KERENSKY

In Russia, the war was opposed by many left-wing groups from the beginning. Initially, however, it was supported by the Socialist leader Aleksandr Fyodorovich Kerensky. He had been elected to the fourth Duma in 1912 as a Trudoviki (Labour Group) delegate. In the Duma, he had been regarded by Bolsheviks as a leader of the moderate left, and was instrumental in pushing through such reforms as health insurance for the growing class of industrial workers. Kerensky had a knack for compromising with delegates to his right when it worked to the benefit of his Socialist convictions, but he also "acquired a reputation as the most outspoken critic of the monarchy and its ministers in the entire Duma."[7]

Kerensky's background was neither peasant nor working class. His father was a nobleman, his mother the daughter of a tsarist general. He had been born in Simbirsk, a city on the Volga River, on April 22, 1881. When he was eight years old, the family moved to the Central Asian city of Tashkent, where Aleksandr grew to manhood. In 1899 he left Tashkent to study law at the University of St. Petersburg. While there he met and married Olga Baranovskaya, and joined the Narodniki (Populist) revolutionary movement. Following his graduation, Kerensky joined the Socialist Revolutionary party.

During the 1905 revolution, Kerensky became involved in a plot to assassinate the tsar. He was arrested, but his family had connections in the government, and he got off lightly. His penalty was to be sent back to Tashkent, where his father was director of the school system, and to remain there for several months. Less than a year later, he was back in St. Petersburg.

The incident had made Kerensky a prominent figure in Socialist politics, and when he began to practice law, most of his cases involved defending those who were charged with crimes against the tsarist government. Throughout the early 1900s he defended Polish, Latvian, and Armenian nationalists, as well as Bolsheviks, anarchists, and other revolutionaries. A skilled orator in addition to being a successful attorney, he was in great demand to speak at Socialist meetings.

His popularity ensured his election to the fourth Duma in 1912. He allied himself with the Mensheviks, and soon became one of their leaders. Despite his support for the war, when the tsar had the Bolshevik members of the Duma arrested in 1914, Kerensky defended them in court. He went on to become the tsar's fiercest critic—and eventually one of those who would briefly replace him as head of the Russian government.

THE MOUNTING LOSSES

In 1914 the tsar had more serious problems than Kerensky. With the war barely a month old, a Russian army had tried to invade Prussia and suffered a major defeat at the Battle of Tannenberg. More than 100,000 Russian soldiers had been killed. Unable to face his tsar, the general in command had committed suicide.

Two weeks later, despite an advantage in manpower over the Germans, the Russians suffered a second defeat at Masurian Lakes. The losses were estimated at 125,000 men. Observers reporting back to the tsar "blamed poor leadership, a lack of effective reconnaissance, secrecy and faulty communications."[8]

By May 1915 the Russian armies had lost more than one million men. Much of Poland was in the hands of the Germans. The only thing that saved Russia from complete defeat was the fact that the Schlieffen Plan had not worked. During 1914 the Russian resistance had required the Germans to supply the forces fighting them with reinforcements, which had been intended for the conquest of France. Now French and British troops were dug in facing German trenches, and the battle lines would remain virtually unchanged throughout most of the war.

Tsar Nicholas was now beset from all sides. There were a mounting number of peace demonstrations throughout Russia. The war was under attack daily in the Duma. Kerensky, who had once supported it, was now leading the opposition. Desertions from the army were increasing every day. Neither the tsar's generals nor his advisers could agree on strategy or tactics. He himself did not approve of the conduct of the war by his second cousin Grand Duke Nicholas, whom he had put in charge of the armed forces. He decided to dismiss the grand duke, take over command of his armies himself, and go to the front to lead them.

Virtually all of the tsar's advisers tried to talk him out of this. His Council of Ministers sent him a letter begging him to reconsider. Their opposition was not just out of consideration for his safety. They also feared that with Nicholas gone, "power would pass into the hands of the 'German' Empress [tsarina] and her disreputable confidant," Rasputin.[9]

THE TSAR'S DECISION

The tsarina urged her husband to go and lead his army into battle. His leadership, she assured him, would bring victory. Rasputin's domination over Alexandra colored her advice. With the tsar away, Rasputin's influence and power could only grow. They were the rewards of an intimacy that had been building between him and the tsarina for a long time.

As far back as 1912, a letter from the tsarina to Rasputin had been leaked to the press. The letter had told Rasputin that "I kiss your hands and lay my head upon your blessed shoulders. I feel so joyful then. Then all I want is to sleep, sleep for ever on your shoulder, in your embrace." When the letter appeared, many of the tsar's supporters had urged him to expel Rasputin from the royal court. But he had refused, saying, "Better one Rasputin than ten fits of hysterics every day."[10]

More recently, in March 1915, Rasputin had gone to a restaurant with two journalists and three prostitutes and gotten quite drunk. He began to boast loudly of his intimate relations with the tsarina. "I can make her do anything," he boasted, and he made a coarse gesture.[11] Someone called the police, and when they arrived, Rasputin proclaimed his identity and defiantly dropped his pants as if to prove he was who he said he was. They arrested him anyway, and he spent the night in jail. The next morning, however, he was released on orders from the tsar.

There was, however, no telling how long the tsar would go on closing his eyes to Rasputin's disgraceful and embarrassing behavior. Rasputin wouldn't have to worry about that if the tsar went to the front. With the tsar away, Rasputin would flit in like a spider to take over the web of Imperial Russian government.

AN EXPENSIVE OFFENSIVE

By the time the tsar left to take command of the Russian armed forces, Aleksandr Kerensky had been identified by the secret police as the "chief

Tsar Nicholas II
(on horse) takes command of
the Russian armed forces.

ringleader of the present revolutionary movement."[12] He was the most out-spoken anti-tsarist in the Duma. Following the defeat of the Russian armies in Poland, he secretly organized workers' soviets for revolution and encouraged the sabotaging of the war effort. Rejecting his former pro-war position, he embraced the antiwar resolution drawn up by a coalition of Marxists influenced by Lenin.

Despite his near-treasonous activities, Kerensky was not arrested. In part, this was due to his prominence and popularity with both intellectuals and common people. A greater asset was probably his ability as a coalition-building politician. With the tsar away, the conservatives who had supported Nicholas found themselves more and more under the thumb of the tsarina and her influential adviser Rasputin. Kerensky played a major role in convincing them to join forces with the liberals in the Duma to call for a truly democratic parliament with the power to make laws that neither the tsar nor the tsarina could veto. Such allies, many of them nobles, undoubtedly influenced the police not to arrest Kerensky.

The tsar refused to give up power to a democratic parliament. He ordered that the Duma be adjourned. This sparked protests and heightened the passion for revolution, but the tsar was focused on the war, and out of touch with the extent of discontent on the home front. It had been learned that the German High Command had suspended offensive operations against Russia in order to bolster its forces on the western front. This left the Austro-Hungarians vulnerable. On June 4, 1916, the Russian Army launched a major offensive against them. The operation was successful; lost territory was regained, new territory was seized, 300,000 prisoners were taken, and twice that number were killed or wounded. It was a great victory, but it had cost the lives of another million Russian soldiers.

WORKING WOMEN

The people of Russia did not rejoice. The loss of so many young men had soured them on the war. The loss of the labor of the millions of young men serving in the army translated into reduced crop production. Crops that were picked were rotting because the army had taken over the railroads to transport munitions, and there was no way to get food to market. As food became scarcer, prices rose. In the cities, ordinary people were caught between inflation and starvation. In October 1916 the Department of Police "warned that another revolution could be in the offing."[13]

Women and children were particularly hard hit. At this time 33 percent of the workforce in Russian factories were women. Many small children were also employed. Men in Russian factories were paid less than anywhere else in the industrialized world. Even so, it was cheaper to hire women and children because they could be paid still less. "A woman worker of fifty sees and hears poorly, her head trembles, her shoulders are sharply hunched over," wrote a Russian factory doctor. "She looks about seventy."[14] If her husband was not in the army, he was less likely to have a job than she was. He was also likely to be an alcoholic and to beat her. Alcoholism and spouse abuse were common problems in tsarist Russia.

Some women, those not too beaten down, were attracted to the growing movement for revolution. There were strikes in the factories, and women workers walked out with the men. Other women wrote letters to their husbands in the army, encouraging them to desert. There were many such desertions, and there were more mutinies as well. In the universities the intellectuals were openly demanding an end to the war, and an end to tsarist tyranny.

THE QUESTION

Hoping to avoid imminent revolution, the tsar's ministers allowed the Duma to reconvene on November 1, 1916. Kerensky made an impassioned speech charging the tsarist government with "filling its prisons with working people." He then thundered that one man was responsible for the Russian nightmare: "Grisha Rasputin."[15]

There was good reason for the accusation. With the tsar away, Alexandra had asserted her royal right to rule in his place. Her letters to Nicholas were filled with advice from "Our Friend," or the "holy peasant," meaning Rasputin. She told Nicholas to base his war strategy on what Rasputin had "seen in the night." She passed along to the tsar advice from Rasputin on arms transport, food rations, finance, and land reform.[16]

Rasputin's influence was even greater when it came to replacing government ministers with men who would do his bidding. If they balked at some of his demands, Rasputin would whisper in the tsarina's ear, and they, too, would be replaced. In the months after the tsar left for the front, Russia had four prime ministers, five ministers of the interior, three foreign ministers, three war ministers, three ministers of transport, and four ministers of agriculture. Most were answerable to the will of Rasputin as passed on to the tsar via Alexandra.

As if the truth was not bizarre enough, rumors and distortions followed. It was said that "the Tsarina and Rasputin were working for the Germans; that they had a direct line to Berlin; and that Nicholas regularly warned his uncle, the Kaiser Wilhelm, of the movements of his troops." The rumors spread like wildfire, and soldiers at the front heard that there was an agreement "to sell the western half of Russia to the enemy."[17]

Those aristocrats loyal to the tsar didn't necessarily believe the rumors. Whether they were true or not, however, something had to be done about the man with the mystical powers who was most responsible for them. Rasputin would have to be terminated. But these were superstitious times, and there was a nagging question:

Was Rasputin a man who could be killed?

CHAPTER
SEVEN

THE FALL OF THE
DYNASTY

> **We do not take defeat amiss,**
> **And victory gives us no delight.**
> **The source of all our cares is this:**
> **Can we get vodka for tonight?**
>
> Anonymous lyric sung by war-weary
> St. Petersburg aristocrats in 1916

As the war ground on, and revolution loomed ever closer on the horizon, the Russian aristocracy plunged deeper and deeper into denial. British historian Orlando Figes records that "the rich and high-born lost themselves in a last desperate binge of personal pleasure. They drank their stocks of champagne, spent huge sums of money on black-market caviar, sturgeon and other peacetime delicacies, threw lavish parties, deceived their wives and husbands, and gambled away fortunes in casinos."[1] One prominent nobleman who did not have his head in the sand, however, was Prince Felix Iusopov, heir to the greatest fortune in Russia, and husband of the tsar's niece, Grand Duchess Irena.

THE PLAN

Prince Felix believed that the only way to save Imperial Russia was to kill Rasputin, and then confine the tsarina in a mental institution. Once free of the evil influence of the tsarina and Rasputin, the tsar would presumably agree to a constitutional monarchy. If he didn't agree, the plan was to depose him and replace him with another royal Romanov. The important thing was that revolution be avoided and the monarchy preserved.

Four other people were recruited for the murder by Prince Felix. They were Vladimir Purishkevich, leader of the right wing in the Duma; Grand Duke Dimitry Pavlovich, a favorite nephew of the tsar; a mysterious Dr. Lazavert; and a young army lieutenant whose identity has been lost to history. All agreed to participate in the murder.

Late in the evening of December 16, 1916, Rasputin was lured to the home of Prince Felix to meet the prince's young and beautiful wife. Rasputin, assuming from his past experiences in the decadent royal court that Prince Felix would have no objection to his wife being seduced, was quick to accept the invitation. He did so even though he had been warned that he would be assassinated if he went to the Iusopov palace.

Grand Duchess Irena was actually a thousand miles away in the country. Prince Felix's co-conspirators, however, were in the room directly above the chamber where Rasputin and Prince Felix were supposedly awaiting her appearance. While they waited, Prince Felix offered his guest some pastries and wine. Both were laced with powerful doses of potassium cyanide, which was supposed to kill Rasputin no more than fifteen minutes after he consumed it.

THE EXECUTION

To entertain his guest, who was growing impatient for Grand Duchess Irena to appear, Prince Felix "set up a gramophone and played the only record they had, 'I'm a Yankee Doodle Dandy,' over and over."[2] Rasputin ate some cakes and drank some Madeira wine. Time passed. Nothing happened. He seemed unaffected by the cyanide.

Prince Felix excused himself and went upstairs to confer with his co-conspirators. Why was Rasputin not dead? There was some talk of his alleged supernatural powers. Perhaps they should just let him go. Instead, Prince Felix borrowed Grand Duke Dimitry's revolver and went back downstairs.

Rasputin was bent over an elaborate old crucifix made of silver and rock crystal, examining it. Prince Felix fired, and Rasputin screamed and dropped to the floor. The other conspirators rushed downstairs. Everybody assumed that Rasputin was dead. Grand Duke Dimitry, Dr.

Lazavert, and the young lieutenant left then, taking Rasputin's overcoat and boots in order to dispose of them. Prince Felix and Purishkevich went into another room to wait for their return so they could then dispose of Rasputin's corpse.

THE LIVING DEAD

Seized by a sudden fear that Rasputin's occult powers might have saved him, and that he wasn't really dead, Prince Felix went in to check on Rasputin's body. It lay perfectly still. Then, suddenly, the left eye twitched and opened. The right eye opened. Rasputin stared at the prince with murderous hatred. Then he was on his feet, seizing Prince Felix by the throat. "Felix! Felix!" he screamed.[3]

Breaking away, Prince Felix ran into the next room where Purishkevich sat smoking a cigar. Almost incoherent, he blurted out that Rasputin was still alive. Purishkevich took the gun and went into the chamber to find Rasputin gone. However, he could hear him shouting outside: "Felix, Felix, I will tell everything to the Empress!"[4]

Purishkevich went out and saw Rasputin staggering through the snow in the garden toward the gate. He fired at him and missed. He fired a second time and missed again. Then he moved closer and fired a third shot. Rasputin fell to the ground. Purishkevich bent over him and shot him again. Then, still fearful that he might be alive, Purishkevich kicked him in the head. Prince Felix, still hysterical, joined him and beat the body with a truncheon.

When the other conspirators returned, they loaded Rasputin's body into a car and drove to a remote spot on the Malaia Moika canal. They weighted down the corpse with chains and tossed it into the water. The evening had so upset them, though, that they neglected to take precautions to keep the killing secret.

Before morning, news of Rasputin's death had spread. Many people did not believe it. They did not think the mystical monk was a man who could be slain. On the afternoon after the murder, Alexandra wrote Tsar Nicholas that "I cannot & *won't* believe He has been killed."[5] When Rasputin's body washed up, crowds of his disciples, including many aristocrats, gathered to collect the water made holy by washing over Rasputin's flesh.

DEPRESSION AND DANGER

The rest of the plan fell apart. Tsar Nicholas was appalled at the murder. "I am ashamed before Russia," he said, "that the hands of my relations should be smeared with the blood of this peasant."[6] Tsarina Alexandra was not committed to an asylum. On the contrary, the tsar drew closer to his wife, and came to depend even more on her advice. When he learned that his nephew, Grand Duke Dmitry Pavlovich, had been involved in the murder, he ordered him to Persia to fight with the Russian Army. Prince Felix was exiled to his estate. None of the assassins ever stood trial. Tsar Nicholas's mother, the dowager empress, persuaded her son not to prosecute them because of their connection to the royal family.

Rasputin's assassination deepened the tsar's despair. The repeated defeats of his armies had caused him to have frequent periods of depression, insomnia, and anxiety. Rasputin had supplied Alexandra with sedatives for him. They were said to contain hashish.

The tsar had good reason to be even more upset following Rasputin's death. Reports from the secret police indicated that it was only the beginning of a terrorist campaign designed to lead to the assassination of the tsar himself. As of Christmas 1916, many separate and unrelated plots to kill Nicholas were brewing.

For security reasons, the tsar joined his family at the Alexander Palace in Tsarkoe Selo for Christmas. They did not exchange gifts with their relations back in St. Petersburg. As far as Nicholas and Alexandra were concerned, relatives were no longer to be trusted.

WINTER OF DISCONTENT

Far from the capital city of St. Petersburg, the tsar received information from his advisers designed to reassure him. Bad news, and there was plenty of it as the new year started, was filtered out. He knew that there were plots against him, but he believed that the majority of the people, the 80 percent peasant population of Russia, regarded him as a benevolent ruler who loved them. Alexandra confirmed this, reminding him that the "holy peasant" Rasputin had always said that it was so.

Nicholas didn't recognize the extent of his people's hardship. It was "the coldest winter Russia had experienced for several years." Snow and ice and frozen tracks had brought railway traffic to a standstill. Some of the troops had no weapons because the ammunition trains could not reach them. In many farm districts, the people could not get to market to buy food. There was a severe shortage of food and fuel in the cities. During February, the average temperature in St. Petersburg was "fifteen degrees below zero." Women stood on line all night to buy a loaf of bread. As the supply of flour was used up, many bakeries were forced to close. Rumors spread that the closings were done deliberately in order to force up the price of bread. Fights broke out and shop windows were smashed. Jews were blamed and attacked in the streets. When the government announced that food would be rationed, there were rumors that the aristocrats would get preferential treatment. There was panic buying, and the violence increased.[7]

The weather was key to what followed. A warm spell swept in on March 8. Coincidentally, that was also International Women's Day. A march was held, described by an onlooker as made up of "ladies from society, lots more peasant women, student girls and . . . not many workers." By afternoon, however, they were joined by striking women textile workers who began chanting "Down with the tsar!" and demanding "Bread!" Soon they were joined by male workers. The throng grew to 100,000. Cossacks tried to break up the crowd, but failed.[8]

REBELLION AND ROSES

The protests continued. The next day the crowd grew to 150,000, the day after to 200,000. By then all of the city's major factories had ceased operation. Shops and restaurants were closed. Newspapers failed to publish. Red flags and banners began to appear. Their slogans demanded an end to the war, and the removal of the tsar. Late in the day, not far from where demonstrators had been killed on Bloody Sunday in 1905, the protest march was blocked by a squadron of heavily armed Cossacks with their whips, sabers, and guns at the ready.

They brought the crowd to a standstill. Would the Cossacks charge? Would they fire? Suddenly a young girl walked forward, toward the Cossacks. She opened her cloak to reveal a bunch of red roses. She held it up to the commanding officer on his horse. The officer smiled. He leaned down and accepted the flowers. The crowd applauded and shouted its approval.

It was the first sign that the military would not protect the government. There were others. Some soldiers not only refused to fire on the demonstrators, but they actually joined them in fighting the police. In one incident, Cossacks attacked the mounted police that were attacking protesters. The commander of the police was killed, run through with a Cossack saber. In another instance, soldiers mutinied and fired on other soldiers who were attacking the crowd. As one young sergeant said, "It would be better to die with honour than to obey any further orders to shoot at the crowds."[9]

The Bolsheviks played no part in any of this. Lenin was in Switzerland. Stalin was en route from Siberia to St. Petersburg. Trotsky, having been thrown out of France for his radical activities, was in New York City. They did not believe Russia was ready for a revolution. The leading Bolshevik in St. Petersburg told a Socialist meeting held by Kerensky that there "will be no revolution."[10]

THE THREAT OF ANARCHY

Nevertheless, the soldiers' mutinies spread. Troops led the crowds in opening the prisons. In early March, a crowd of 25,000 marched on the Duma. They were greeted by Menshevik leaders, including Kerensky. The Mensheviks announced that they had formed a Provisional Executive Committee of the Soviet of Workers' Deputies. They asked the crowd to elect representatives to attend the first meeting of the Soviet that evening.

However, there was little control of the voting procedures. The workers were not organized to function politically. When three thousand delegates assembled, more than two thirds were members of the armed forces. Most of them were young peasants whose families—thanks to the Stolypin reforms—often owned farmland. They were more easily influenced by conservative views of private property than by Socialist arguments.

Meanwhile, moderate Duma members were reluctant to hand over power to the radicals and their followers. They had received an order from the tsar to dissolve the Duma altogether. They hesitated, and then formed the Temporary Committee of the Duma with the aim of restoring order in St. Petersburg. However, they didn't have the power to do this. When some four thousand tsarist government officials were seized by the crowd, the Temporary Committee caved in and ordered that more officials be arrested and turned over to the Duma for justice.

Both the Soviet leaders and the Temporary Committee were now fearful that the revolution might dissolve in anarchy. Crowds were roaming the St. Petersburg streets, vandalizing shops and looting homes, particularly those of the rich. Violence was everywhere. There was similar turmoil in other Russian cities. Soldiers were deserting the battlefields, and many were joining the bands of looters roving over rural areas. Before anything could be accomplished, order had to be restored.

To do that, the radicals joined the moderates to establish a bourgeoisie government. However, they also had another reason. It was Marxist doctrine, which all on the left—including the Bolsheviks—accepted, that in a backward country like Russia there would have to be a long period of capitalism before the workers would be advanced enough for a proletarian revolution. In other words, those who worked for wages would have to be exploited by those who owned the means of production before their consciousness was raised enough for them to successfully rebel. So the idea—bizarre as it sounds—was to create a capitalist democracy in order to eventually overthrow it.

BIRTH OF THE KERENSKY CULT

On March 14, 1917, a small group formed jointly by the Soviet of Workers' Deputies and the Temporary Committee of the Duma met to work out a program for governing before anarchy consumed Russia. They laid out certain principles, including amnesty for political prisoners; freedom of speech, press, and assembly; abolition of restrictions based on class, religion, and nationality; a guarantee that troops who had supported the revolution would not be sent to the front; creation of a people's militia with elected officers; and—most important of all—the immediate convening of a constituent assembly to determine the form of government of the country. The meeting did not resolve the question of whether or not Russia should withdraw from the war.

An interim cabinet was set up to run the government while it was being decided what form that government should take. There were twelve members. Six of them were members of the Masonic Order, a secret fraternal society with chapters throughout the world. This raised the question of how active a role Masons played in the Russian Revolution. That question has never been answered.

Two of the Masons were Kerensky and Prince Georgii Lvov, who had been selected as the prime minister of what was now called the Provisional Government. Prince Lvov was a liberal aristocrat who had championed self-government in Russian provinces in place of the often tyrannical rule by governors appointed by the tsar. He was known nationwide as a reformer and was popular with the people. He owed allegiance to no party, and because of his abilities as a conciliator, he was acceptable to all.

Kerensky was named minister of justice. Thirty-five years old, he was already a leading Socialist figure regarded by the St. Petersburg crowds as their representative. The Bolsheviks, however, questioned his revolutionary zeal. They noticed that he had worn a morning-coat and starched collar in the Duma but ripped them off when he spoke to the workers' Soviet. As Trotsky put it, Kerensky only "hung around the revolution."[11] Nevertheless, there was no denying Kerensky's leadership skills as a speaker and organizer, and soon he was amassing a large following, which would become known as the Kerensky Cult. To the crowds who adored him, Kerensky and the revolution were one and the same.

THE TSAR ABDICATES

The tsar had returned to the front at the beginning of 1917. By mid-February, the widespread strength of the revolution could no longer be kept from him. He had two reactions. He sent troops to St. Petersburg to punish the rebels and establish a military dictatorship. He himself set out for Tsarkoe Selo to be with his wife and children. Both objectives were foiled.

When the troops he sent to St. Petersburg reached Tsarkoe Selo, the commanding general found that the Imperial Guards stationed there had mutinied. When the tsarina greeted the troops that had just arrived, she was met with surly looks and muttered disapproval. Some of the new

The New York Times.

THE WEATHER
Fair today; tomorrow rain or snow; moderate northwesterly winds.
☞ For full weather report see Page 19

NEW YORK, FRIDAY, MARCH 16, 1917.—TWENTY PAGES.

VOL. LXVI...NO. 21,601.

ONE CENT In Greater New York | TWO CENTS New England and Middle States. | THREE CENTS Elsewhere.

REVOLUTION IN RUSSIA; CZAR ABDICATES; MICHAEL MADE REGENT, EMPRESS IN HIDING; PRO-GERMAN MINISTERS REPORTED SLAIN

RAILWAY STRIKE ORDERED TO BEGIN TOMORROW NIGHT

Managers and Heads of Brotherhoods End Final Conference, Both Defiant.

WILSON NOW THE ONLY HOPE

President Seems to Have No Authority, but May Make Appeal to Patriotism.

FIVE DAYS' GRACE FOR MILK

Travelers to Have Time to Get Home —Appeals for the Public's Approval.

The eight-hour fight between the 230 railroads of the United States and the 400,000 trainmen has placed the country again face to face with a nationwide railway strike.

The National Conference Committee of the Railways yesterday defied the ultimatum of the four brotherhoods that the eight-hour day should be put into effect at once, and the labor chiefs formally served notice that their strike order stood and that a progressive strike program would begin tomorrow night at 5 o'clock. Freight alone will

Government Heads Hold a Mysterious Conference

Special to The New York Times.
WASHINGTON, March 15.—A conference surrounded with much mystery took place late this afternoon in the office of the Secretary of State. In addition to Secretary Lansing, it was attended by Mr. Baker, the Secretary of War; Mr. Gregory, the Attorney General; Mr. Daniels, the Secretary of the Navy; Mr. Polk, the Counsellor of the State Department, and Mr. Woolsey, personal legal adviser to the Secretary of State.

After the conference it was said by one of those who attended it that no particular subject had been discussed. It had been devoted, he indicated, to many questions that naturally came up for discussion at this critical period in the international relations of the United States. Elsewhere, however, the impression was given that the conference was called to consider matters of rather pressing importance.

FRYATT'S FATE FOR OUR GUNNERS

German Threat to Put to Death Crews of Any Armed American Ships They Capture.

WARNING IN MUNICH PAPER

Assumes That President "Realizes Fate to Which He is Subjecting His Artillerymen."

LONDON HAILS REVOLUTION

Expected Czar's Overthrow and Sees Brighter Prospects for the Allies.

THINK THE COUP DECISIVE

Well-Informed Observers Believe the Patriotic War Party Has Made Its Control Secure.

FEAR NO SEPARATE PEACE

With Weak Ruler Deposed and Pro-German Advisers Ousted, They Predict New Victories.

Special Cable to The New York Times.
LONDON, Friday, March 16—It is the belief in well-informed circles here that the Provisional Government which has been set up in Russia by the military party will be able to keep the upper hand in maintaining a policy that means the uninterruptedly vigorous prosecution of the war to a victorious end.

The overthrow of the Czar was expected, and observers here are confident that the Grand Duke as regent will have the solid support of the war party, while they are equally sure of the elimination of any element with a pro-German taint.

Duma Appeals to the Army for Unity Against Foe; Gives Pledge of No Weakening or Suspension of War

LONDON, March 15.—The Reuter correspondent at Petrograd telegraphs under date of yesterday:

"The Military Committee of the Duma has asked all the officers not yet employed by the committee to undertake the organization of the soldiers who joined the people, and help guard the capital. The committee issued a statement, pointing out that at the present moment, when facing an enemy who wished to take advantage of the temporary weakness of the country, it was absolutely necessary to make every effort to maintain the power of the army. It added that the blood of the Russians who had died during the two and a half years of war pledged the people to do this.

"The President of the Duma sent telegrams to the commanders of the Baltic and Black Sea fleets, to the chiefs of the armies on the northern, southwestern, western, Rumanian, and Caucasus fronts, and to the Chief of the General Staff, requesting that the army and navy preserve absolute calm, and to be sure that the struggle against the foreign enemy was not suspended or weakened even for a single moment. The telegrams sent these commanders added:

As hitherto, the army and navy must continue firmly and valiantly to defend the country, and while the Provisional Committee is aided by the military element in the capital and with the moral support of the people in restoring calm and regular activity, each officer, soldier, and sailor should fulfil his duty.

"The officers of the Petrograd garrison at a general meeting unanimously agreed to recognize the authority of the Executive Committee of the Duma until the formation of a permanent Government.

"An imperial bodyguard regiment rode into Petrograd today. It is estimated that there are now 60,000 troops in the capital."

People in Revolt Burn and Slay in Streets of Russia's Capital

Fashionable Hotel Riddled by Machine Guns When Pro-German Shoots at Croud—Count Frederick's Home Set on Fire and Family Ill-Treated—General de Knorring Shot.

Stuermer and Protopopoff Reported Assassinated

Special Cable to The New York Times.
LONDON, Friday, March 16.—

ARMY JOINS WITH THE DUMA

Three Days of Conflict Follow Food Riots in Capital.

POPULACE TAKE UP ARMS

But End Comes Suddenly When Troops Guarding Old Ministers Surrender.

CZAR FINDS CAPITAL GONE

Returns from Front After Receiving Warning from Duma and Gives Up His Throne.

Empress Reported Under Guard or Hiding From Angry People

Special Cable to The New York Times.
PETROGRAD, March 14. (Dispatch to The London Daily Chronicle.)—The Empress of Russia has been placed under guard.

LONDON, March 15.—According to information received here the Russian people have been most distrustful during recent events of the personal influence of Empress Alexandra. She was reputed to exercise the greatest influence over Emperor Nicholas.

It is stated that her whereabouts

Leading Figures in Russian Revolution.

Czar Nicholas II who Has Abdicated

Czarevitch Alexis (L) To who will succeed to the Throne

---

arrivals joined the mutineers. Orders were received from the acting commander in chief of the army in St. Petersburg not to march into the capital city, which was now held by mutinous troops.

Meanwhile, Tsar Nicholas's train had been detoured because of troop movements. Then it was detoured a second time because mutinous troops had seized a section of the rail line. Nicholas had to get off the train in Pskov at 7:00 P.M. on March 14. That same day the tsar received a cable from the commander in chief in St. Petersburg asking him to let the Duma form a government, which would result in a constitutional monarchy. The tsar refused.

Events moved so quickly that they made his refusal meaningless. The Temporary Committee of the Duma had drawn up a resolution demanding that Nicholas abdicate. After the tsar received it, his generals were contacted and asked if they thought he should abdicate. They were unanimous in favor of abdication. The tsar was devastated, but he wrote out his agreement on a telegraph blank. He said he was "prepared to renounce the throne in favor of My Son, with the understanding that He will remain with Me until attaining maturity, and that My Brother, Michael Aleksandrovich will serve as Regent."[12]

His insistence that Tsarevich Alexis remain with him was viewed by some as not just a matter of fatherly affection. It was known that Nicholas had consulted a doctor and been told that there was little chance that twelve-year-old Alexis would live past his sixteenth birthday. With Russia remaining a monarchy, the opponents of Nicholas feared that when Alexis died Nicholas would act to reclaim the throne. They refused to agree to allow the tsarevich to remain with Nicholas.

There was already a strong movement among the Soviets to end the monarchy altogether. The people were increasingly in favor of doing away with it. Even among the peasants, who were traditionally pro-tsarist, the hardships of war had created an antimonarchy sentiment.

To avoid ending the monarchy, the Provisional Government wanted an immediate abdication to put the tsar's son on the throne with Nicholas's brother, Grand Duke Michael, as regent to advise and act for him. They felt that they could control both Michael and the tsarevich so long as the boy was kept separate from his father. They were foiled when the tsar announced that he had decided to abdicate for himself and for the tsarevich as well. This meant that the crown would pass to the tsar's brother.

Tsar Nicholas abdicated on March 15, 1917. The next day his brother refused the crown. Grand Duke Michael also signed abdication papers. In the midst of chaos and ongoing revolution, the three hundred years of Romanov rule of Imperial Russia had come to an end.

CHAPTER
EIGHT

THE REDS SEIZE
POWER

> The Soviets are the most perfect representatives of the people—perfect in their revolutionary experience, in their ideas and objects. Based directly upon the army in the trenches, the workers in the factories, and the peasants in the fields, they are the backbone of the Revolution.
>
> Leon Trotsky, 1917

In the spring of 1917, there was good news and bad news for the German kaiser. The good news was the tsar's abdication and the turmoil in Russia. The bad news was the April 6 declaration of war on Germany by the United States. Since 1914, German troops had been locked in a stalemate with Britain and France costing millions of lives. Now came the threat of United States troops tipping the balance against Germany. The German armies tied up on the Russian front were desperately needed to stave off defeat. However, the Russian Provisional Government had decided to continue fighting them. The German High Command believed that decision might be changed by Vladimir Lenin.

SLEEPING WITH THE ENEMY

In Zurich, Switzerland, Lenin had observed events in Russia with considerable frustration. The March riots sparked a change of mind regarding Marxist doctrine. They indicated to him that Russian workers and peasants were ready for a truly Marxist revolution. What was lacking was Bolshevik leadership. The Provisional Government was far from Marxist. Lenin considered Prince Lvov a figurehead, and Kerensky the real power behind a government, which would leave the landowning aristocracy and the wealthy industrialists in place while continuing to fight the war. The *real* revolution, Lenin believed, had yet to be made.

The Germans viewed Lenin as "much more raving mad" than Kerensky.[1] They saw Lenin as a charismatic leader of antiwar radicals who would spread the anarchy that would destroy Russia's ability to wage war. It was in their interest to help Lenin return to Russia.

A deal was reached. The German High Command supplied Lenin with gold "worth between $6 and $10 million" to be used to help destabilize the present Russian regime.[2] One of Lenin's conditions was that there be no hint that he was pro-German or a traitor to the Russian people. The Germans went along with this by "sealing him in a railroad car and guiding it through the battlefields of Europe."[3] He was accompanied by thirty-one other radical Russians including Grigori Zinoviev. Not all were Bolsheviks. At least three were followers of Trotsky, who was still not committed to Lenin's policies. On April 9 they left Zurich bound for the German frontier. Then, via Germany, Sweden, and Finland, Lenin arrived in St. Petersburg on April 16, 1917. It was a Bolshevik day to remember.

DICTATORSHIP OF THE PROLETARIAT

At this time, the membership of the Russian Bolshevik party was dwindling. The Bolsheviks had played no real role in getting rid of the tsar and setting up the Provisional Government. To the general population, Kerensky was the man of the hour, and Lenin a distant figure. However, in an effort to rebuild Bolshevik ranks, an All-Russian Bolshevik Conference was being held in St. Petersburg on the very day that Lenin arrived.

When his train pulled into St. Petersburg's Finland Station, a crowd of Bolsheviks from all over Russia met it. Their ranks were swelled by workers from the Soviets. An honor guard of revolutionary soldiers stood at attention. As Lenin emerged from the train, a band struck up the "Marseillaise." Outside the station, Lenin climbed up on an armored car. Projector lamps lit his face as he urged the crowd to "worldwide Socialist revolution."[4] Then, amid a flurry of red flags, Lenin was escorted to Bolshevik headquarters in the palace of a former mistress of the tsar's.

The next day Lenin addressed an assembly of Social Democrats. He stunned them by calling for a new revolution, which would put power directly in the hands of the people. He told them that those presently in power were weak, and that their aims were bourgeois. It was time for the Soviets to take over. Bolsheviks must be in charge and must establish the "Dictatorship of the Proletariat."[5]

It was a key phrase, one that would be used to justify Communist tyranny over the next seventy years. It meant rule in the name of the people by the few who selected themselves to rule them. The Soviets would rule the people. The Central Committee would rule the Soviets. The party chairman would rule the Central Committee. It would not be a dictatorship by the people; it would be a dictatorship imposed on the people by one person.

SOCIALISM VS. PATRIOTISM

The lines were drawn. The Bolsheviks would not support the Provisional Government. Later that day, Lenin delivered his so-called April Thesis. It demanded transfer of power from the Provisional Government to the workers' Soviets, an end to the war, confiscation of all property and nationalization of all land, including the small farms owned by peasants, Soviet control of production and distribution, and the creation of a Socialist International to spread the revolution throughout the rest of Europe. The April Thesis lacked popular support and had no likelihood of success at that time, but it was prophetic. Every one of its demands would be realized in the future.

Lenin would accomplish this with the help of his three closest associates, Zinoviev, Stalin, and Trotsky. Zinoviev had accompanied Lenin from Switzerland, and Stalin had arrived in Leningrad shortly before Lenin. Trotsky was in New York City when he learned of the revolution and set out immediately to return to Russia. However, British authorities removed him from his ship at Halifax, Nova Scotia, and forced him to remain in Canada for a month. It was May 4 when he finally arrived in St. Petersburg.

Differences between Trotsky and Lenin had never been resolved, but the situation in St. Petersburg pushed Trotsky toward bolshevism. Like

Lenin, he opposed the war. However, a Russian victory at Lwow on June 16 weakened support for their position. At a Pan-Russian Congress of All Councils of Workmen's and Soldiers' Delegates, Lenin roared that pursuing the war was "treason to the interests of international socialism." Kerensky had again completely reversed his position. Now minister of war, he shouted back that any peace agreement would be "fraternizing with the enemy." The congress voted to continue the war.[6]

The Lwow victory aroused a new patriotism in the Russian people. It was short-lived. The Germans mounted a fierce counteroffensive. Russian troops broke ranks and fled. Soon they were spread over the countryside, looting and spreading panic. At the same time Ukraine, called Russia's breadbasket because it produced so much of its food, revolted and demanded independence.

A TRAITOR REVEALED

Kerensky was now at the front, leading the troops. His popularity with the people rose and fell according to the news of the day. When rumors spread that regiments stationed in St. Petersburg were about to be ordered to the front, Kerensky was accused of "following in the footsteps of 'Nicholas the Bloody.'" Trotsky demanded "the transfer of power to the Soviet." On July 3, soldiers' riots swept over the city. On July 4 five to six thousand armed sailors disembarked in St. Petersburg. They marched to Bolshevik headquarters under a banner reading "All Power to the Soviets." That banner, and others, had been prepared by the Bolshevik Central Committee.[7]

With Kerensky at the front, the Provisional Government in St. Petersburg was in effect held captive. Bolshevik influence on the Soviets made a takeover seem imminent. It was prevented when a high official of the Provisional Government met with eighty representatives of military units stationed in St. Petersburg and journalists from all the St. Petersburg newspapers. He showed them evidence that Lenin was collaborating with the Germans.

The disclosure spread quickly through the rank and file of soldiers, sailors, and workers in St. Petersburg. Whether they favored the Bolsheviks, the Soviets, or the Provisional Government, "they felt passionately about collaboration with the enemy." Lenin had to ask the soviets to protect him. Loyal troops dispersed the crowds surrounding the buildings where the Provisional Government had been cornered. The sailors returned to their ships. On July 17, Lenin and the other Bolshevik leaders were charged with "high treason and organizing an armed uprising."[8]

Lenin fled to Finland. Stalin and Zinoviev went into hiding. Trotsky was arrested and went to prison. While there, he decided to put aside his doubts about Lenin and commit himself to Bolshevism. When the Bolsheviks held their Sixth Congress at the end of July, Trotsky's followers, at his urging, attended, pledged their support, and joined the party.

THE ARROGANT GENERAL

Although the government had survived the July riots, the prime minister, Prince Lvov, was badly shaken by them. He felt that the days of his government were numbered. Predicting chaos and seeing no way out, he resigned on July 20 and named Kerensky as his successor. The prince then retired to a monastery.

Kerensky was afraid that the ongoing turmoil would lead to a counterrevolution that would restore the monarchy. Because of this, he believed that the support of the Bolsheviks and the workers' Soviets might one day be important to him. With this in mind, he did not retaliate strongly against those involved in the July disturbances. He was strongly criticized for this by General Lavr Georgyevich Kornilov, the new commander in chief of the Russian armies.

General Kornilov had been appointed to the post by Kerensky on August 1, 1917. It was part of Kerensky's strategy to straddle the fence between his opponents on the right and left. Kornilov, described as "small and agile, with a closely shaven head, Mongol mustache and little mousy eyes," was considered "a champion of their cause" by monarchists and other right-wing groups.[9]

Soon after his appointment, Kornilov announced that he was responsible only to his "conscience and to the nation as a whole."[10] It was an open challenge to Kerensky's authority. Kornilov then made a number of demands, the most drastic of which was the imposition of martial law throughout the country. By now many of Kornilov's supporters were urging him to do away with the Provisional Government altogether. There were secret plans being drawn up for a coup d'etat—a military takeover of the government. On August 10, Kornilov went to Kerensky's headquarters in the St. Petersburg Winter Palace with two soldiers armed with machine guns and threatened violence if his demands were not met.

KERENSKY PREVAILS

Kornilov's arrogance grew by leaps and bounds over the following days. The monarchists were supporting him openly and not hesitating to show their disdain for Kerensky. At first, Kerensky was in despair, but finally he acted. He gave up his balancing act between left and right. He used the newspapers to expose Kornilov as a traitor to the Provisional Government. He persuaded the workers' Soviets to help him foil a right-wing plot by setting up the Special Committee for Struggle Against the Counter Revolution. He enlisted the Mensheviks and other left-wing parties to support the government. Kerensky released Trotsky and other Bolsheviks from jail to help save the revolution. They organized the workers' Soviets and the soldiers in the St. Petersburg garrisons to defend the capital against Kornilov's forces.

The sailors who had participated in the July riots returned to protect the Provisional Government. Trade unions organized to guard their factories against a Kornilov takeover. The final blow to Kornilov was when his troops, not eager to be used to bring down the revolutionary government, began to defect. One unit of cavalry hoisted a red flag bearing the words "Land and Freedom," arrested their commanders, and sent word to St. Petersburg pledging loyalty to Kerensky.

In the end there was no battle, and very few shots were fired. Even the Cossacks joined the pro-Kerensky forces. Kornilov was arrested and sent to prison. The Kerensky Cult had prevailed—but not for long.

BOLSHEVISM ON THE RISE

A major result of the Kornilov affair was that it established the Bolsheviks as a political force. Workers, soldiers, and sailors who felt that neither the government, the Mensheviks, nor the other Socialist parties were effective, turned in droves to the Bolsheviks. Their ranks rose to 350,000 members. Many more nonmembers followed the Bolshevik party lead. By mid-September 1917, Bolsheviks had won control of the Soviets in both St. Petersburg and Moscow. Trotsky was elected chairman of the St. Petersburg Soviets. In Moscow, in the city Duma elections, Bolsheviks won 51 percent of the vote.

The most popular promise of the Bolsheviks was that they would end the war in which Russia was continuing to suffer defeats. There was a real danger now that the Germans might mount an offensive to take St. Petersburg. When the government made plans to move the Russian capital to Moscow, it stirred up rumors that "Kerensky meant to surrender Petrograd [St. Petersburg] to the Germans in order to defuse the [Bolshevik] revolution."[11]

Lenin had returned to St. Petersburg secretly on October 20. On October 23, at his urging, the Bolshevik Central Committee voted "to place armed insurrection on the agenda."[12] Only two members opposed the motion. One of them was Zinoviev. He was against seizing power from the Kerensky government. Although Zinoviev would enjoy great power under Lenin, the Bolshevik leader would always refer to Zinoviev as the "strike-breaker of the Revolution."[13]

ALL POWER TO THE SOVIETS

The main asset of the Bolsheviks now was their control of the Soviets. Muscle was provided by the Soldiers' Section of the St. Petersburg Soviet. On October 30, representatives of the St. Petersburg regiments announced that the "garrison no longer recognizes the Provisional Government."[14] They added that they would obey only the orders of the St. Petersburg Soviet.

A congress of Soviets from all over Russia was scheduled to meet in St. Petersburg on November 7. Lenin decided that "we must act on the seventh, the day the Congress meets, so that we may say to it, 'Here is the power! What are you going to do with it?'"[15]

Unwittingly, Kerensky took an action that meshed with Lenin's schedule. Believing he could avert revolution by shutting off the flood of propa-

ЦАРЬ, ПОП И БОГАЧ

НА ПЛЕЧАХ У ТРУДОВОГО НАРОДА.

A Bolshevik propaganda poster showing "The Old Regime" in which beleaguered workers are pictured carrying the tsar, a priest, and a capitalist

ganda in the city, on the morning of November 6 he dispatched soldiers to shut down the Bolshevik newspapers and printing presses. However, when they were met by troops sympathetic to the Bolsheviks and by Red Guard units organized by the Soviets, the forces of the Provisional Government simply faded away. By evening most of the city was in the hands of the Bolsheviks and their allies. The Bolsheviks then directed a deliberate takeover of public utilities and government buildings.

On the morning of November 7, 1917, the leading Bolshevik newspaper ran a huge headline: "ALL POWER TO THE SOVIETS OF WORKERS, SOLDIERS, AND PEASANTS! PEACE! BREAD! LAND!"[16] The accompanying article was by Zinoviev. Even as the paper was circulating, Kerensky was fleeing the Winter Palace to go into hiding.

Later that day the Bolshevik forces laid siege to the Winter Palace. As night fell, they forced their way in and took prisoner the government ministers they found there. They proclaimed the overthrow of the Provisional Government. The almost bloodless Bolshevik revolution was over. The Bolsheviks had control of the government, but they still had to establish rule over the rest of the vast country. Nevertheless, the first Communist government in the history of the world was in place.

CHAPTER NINE

CIVIL WAR

> Not a single great revolution in history
> has taken place without civil war.
>
> Vladimir Lenin, September 1917

The seizure of power by the Bolsheviks was endorsed by the Congress of Soviets. In turn, the Bolsheviks proclaimed the Soviets to be the ruling agencies in Russia. They would be represented by the Soviet Central Executive Committee, which was supposed to function as a sort of parliament. The Executive Committee would be the source of power for the Council of People's Commissars, a cabinet made up of heads of the various branches of the government. Lenin was the chairman of the Council of People's Commissars.

In theory, this was the structure that would carry out the will of the people. In actuality, it was the means by which Lenin established an iron grip over the people by placing Bolshevik loyalists in positions of power and by manipulating key leaders of the Soviets. His title of chairman disguised a power to rule as absolute as the tsar's had been. Under him, Stalin was made commissar of nationalities, and Trotsky became commissar of foreign affairs.

THE TREATY OF BREST-LITOVSK

Lenin immediately issued decrees. Private ownership of land was abolished. Control of industry was granted to the Soviets. Banks were nationalized. Tsarist courts were replaced by Soviet-appointed judges. Workers' militias replaced police forces. Titles, class privileges, and inheritances were abolished. Separation of church and state was decreed. Equality of women with men was legally established.

An immediate armistice, and a peace "without annexations or indemnities" was announced.[1] The Bolshevik government ended hostilities against Germany and her allies on November 26, 1917. An armistice was signed at Brest-Litovsk on December 15. This was a violation of the Treaty of London, in which Russia had pledged not to make a separate peace, and there were immediate protests from France, Britain, and the United States.

They were ignored. Negotiations at Brest-Litovsk for a permanent peace began on December 22 with Leon Trotsky representing Russia. Germany's demands were harsh. The German Army had occupied considerable Russian territory in the war, and Germany intended to keep it. Trotsky's strategy was to stall. He was banking on the revolution spreading to Germany. Lenin himself had said that the Bolshevik revolution was "only a preliminary step toward a similar revolution everywhere."[2]

By January 2, 1918, the kaiser's patience had run out. He warned Russia that he would use the "iron fist and shining sword" if German demands were not met.[3] Trotsky responded that Russia would pursue a policy of "neither war nor peace."[4] In other words, Russia would not wage war, but would also not give up territory to Germany. On February 18, Germany renewed military aggression against Russia. German troops were soon within 80 miles (130 kilometers) of St. Petersburg, causing the Bolshevik government to flee to Moscow, a move that proved to be permanent.

Russia now had no choice. On March 3 the Bolsheviks signed a treaty that gave the Germans all they demanded. The terms reduced Russia's population by one third. It gave Germany "32 percent of Russia's cultivable [farming] land, 27 percent of her railways, 54 percent of her industry, and 89 percent of her coal mines."[5]

DUBIOUS DECISIONS

Other things were happening during negotiations at Brest-Litovsk. A major issue following the Bolshevik takeover was whether Socialist parties to the left and right of the Bolsheviks—the Mensheviks, the Socialist-

Revolutionary Combat Organization (SR), the anarchists, the Social Democrats, and others—should participate in the new government. Many Bolsheviks, including Zinoviev, insisted that they be included. When Lenin successfully opposed their inclusion, it caused a split in the Bolshevik party. Zinoviev resigned from the party's Central Committee.

Additional turmoil surrounded Lenin's abolition of farm ownership. This was widely misunderstood by the majority of peasants serving in the army. It caused "a homeward rush of soldiers" eager to claim the land of their former landlords.[6] They did not understand that the land was now owned by the nation as a whole, and that nobody could stake an individual claim to it.

The Bolsheviks had also made a serious error on November 15, 1917, when they issued the *Declaration of the Rights of Peoples*, which said that territories of the former tsarist empire "had the right to secede and set up independent states."[7] Lenin and Trotsky hoped they would rise up against their local governments and join the Bolshevik revolution. However, Finland, Poland, Lithuania, Latvia, and Estonia all became independent nations with no signs of embracing bolshevism. On January 10, 1918, the independent Republic of the Don, homeland to the Cossacks, was announced. More seriously, Belorussia and Ukraine—the breadbasket of the nation—had claimed independence from Russia before the Bolsheviks took power. Indeed, Ukraine had signed a separate peace with the Germans on February 9, a fact that had helped persuade Lenin that if they didn't give in to the German terms, they would be "signing a death warrant for the Soviet regime within three weeks."[8]

START OF THE COUNTERREVOLUTION

An immediate result of the Bolshevik revolution was the counterrevolution. By May 1918, this counterrevolution had broken out in several places at once, and involved different groups with different agendas and leaders. Social Democrats and other political groups barred from the Bolshevik government became part of it. Ethnic groups seizing an opportunity to break the hold of Russian dominance joined it. Aristocrats, landowners, and Imperial Russian army commanders formed a nucleus, and loyal troops followed them. Many who had regarded the tsar as a spiritual leader viewed bolshevism as godless and heretic, a force to be destroyed. Bolshevism was viewed as harsh and unyielding, and peasants were more interested in owning their own small farms than in being part of some scheme for state ownership of land. Collectively the counterrevolutionaries were known as the White Russian forces.

The task of organizing an effective opposition to the White Russians went to Trotsky. After Brest-Litovsk, he had been named commissioner of military affairs, and introduced national conscription. Eight hundred thousand men were drafted into a new Red army organized to fight in the counterrevolution.

They could not be trained and deployed in time, however, to deal with the Czechoslovak Legion, roughly 60,000 volunteers who had joined the Russian army before the revolution to fight the Germans. The Bolsheviks had tried to expel them from Russia via the Trans-Siberian Railway. Instead, the Czechs seized control of the railroad, joined forces with anti-Bolshevik Social Democrats, and set up two regional governments, one in Samara and the other in Omsk, Siberia.

Meanwhile, as early as January 1918, the leader of the Don Cossack troops, General Alexis Kaledin, had vowed to fight the Bolsheviks. So many of his troops deserted to the other side, however, that even the undermanned Red Guard of those early days was able to keep him from making any headway. When his own officers denounced him as ineffective, on February 11, 1918, General Kaledin committed suicide.

A Cossack retreat known as the Ice March followed.[9] It joined up with 7,000 troops fighting a Bolshevik force of 17,000. They were commanded by General Lavr Kornilov, the former Imperial army commander in chief who had led the failed coup against Kerensky. He had somehow gotten out of prison and recruited a White Russian army. His leadership ended when a Bolshevik shell struck his farmhouse headquarters, igniting a fire that consumed him.

STALIN VS. TROTSKY

The Ice March continued, its ranks swelled by Kornilov's shaken troops. It ended in April when new anti-Bolshevik uprisings broke out. In May, the Don Cossacks were reorganized by a new commander, Peter Krasnov. He led them in a series of victories, which cut the supply route to the new Bolshevik capital of Moscow.

Lenin assigned Stalin to reopen the supply route. Key to doing that was the garrison city of Tsaritsyn on the Volga River. (Tsaritsyn would later be renamed Stalingrad.) Stalin arrived in Tsaritsyn on June 6 and found a "bacchanalia of profiteering," black market operations involving outright stealing and reselling at inflationary prices, by army officers and shopkeepers.[10] Many of the officers of the Tsaritsyn garrison had formerly served in the tsarist army. They were professional soldiers whom Trotsky had put in positions of leadership to whip the Red army into shape. Now they were using their positions to profit from the black market, selling off the very food supplies blocked from reaching Moscow. Stalin cracked down hard on the black market. He set ceilings for food prices and established rationing standards. He removed the local military commanders and replaced them with reliable Bolsheviks.

Trotsky was in charge of the military command structure. He became enraged when Stalin's men ignored his orders. The final straw was when Stalin wrote Lenin that "for the good of the cause, I must have military powers." As for Trotsky's authority, Stalin added that "naturally the absence of a piece of paper from Trotsky won't stop me."[11]

While Lenin mediated between the two, Stalin's Bolshevik commanders acted. They had 80,000 men at their disposal, soldiers who had been immobilized by no more than 9,000 of Peter Krasnov's Cossacks while their former commanders put off fighting in favor of profiteering. The Red army struck before the 40,000 reinforcements Krasnov was expecting could reach him. The Cossacks retreated, the supply routes to Moscow were reopened, and Stalin got full credit for saving the new Russian capital.

It was the beginning of a lifelong feud between Stalin and Trotsky who, at one point, had tried to persuade Lenin to court-martial Stalin. Lenin needed them both. Another crisis was shaping up in July 1918. The Socialist Revolutionaries had rebelled against Lenin, denouncing him as a traitor who sold out Russia to the Germans. They had attracted considerable support in Moscow and St. Petersburg, and on July 6 they attacked government offices in both cities. The German ambassador was assassinated. SR actions continued throughout August. By then, the Bolshevik party had been renamed the Communist party, and the SR had assassinated a member of the Communist Central Committee. This was followed by an attempt on Lenin's life, which left him severely wounded. There were mass retaliations, and over the next few months some 1,300 people were executed in St. Petersburg alone.

EXECUTION OF THE ROMANOVS

Many innocent people died along with the rebels. It was not Bolshevik policy to separate the innocent from the guilty. This was made clear in the execution of the Romanovs. Tsar Nicholas, Tsarina Alexandra, and their five children had been held under house arrest at Ekaterinburg in the Ural Mountains. They were confined in a large white house surrounded by a high fence patrolled by sentries. The guards inside the house were surly and sometimes insulting. They went with the tsarina and her daughters to the lavatory and stood outside the door making lewd remarks. Obscenities were scrawled on the walls. The family's personal belongings were stolen. Except for meals, they were confined to their rooms.

In Moscow there were demands to put the tsar on trial and execute him. Lenin resisted them. He did not want to make the tsar a martyr. However, when the Czech Legion surrounded Ekaterinburg at the beginning of July 1918, Lenin was driven to act. There was a real chance the Czechs would liberate the tsar and his family. A live tsar to rally the armed forces of the White Russians was an even worse nightmare for Lenin than a dead martyr. On July 16 a telegram reached Zinoviev from Ekaterinburg and was passed on to Lenin. It said that the Romanovs had to be executed immediately "due to military circumstances."[12] Moscow replied with permission to proceed.

Late in the evening of July 16, the tsar and tsarina, their thirteen-year-old son, Tsarevich Alexis, and his four sisters, Olga, Anastasia, Marie, and Tatiana, were awakened and escorted to a small room in the basement of the house. They were joined by their physician and three servants. The group was told that there was fighting going on outside the house and that they were being moved to the cellar for their protection.

Yakov Yurovsky, one of Lenin's most trusted disciples, entered the room. Behind him in the doorway were eleven armed men. Yurovsky addressed the tsar: "In view of the fact that your relatives are continuing

Before they were taken to Ekaterinburg in April 1918, Tsar Nicholas II and his family were imprisoned at Tobolsk. Nicholas (center) poses with his children on the roof of the prison there, a far cry from the luxury they were accustomed to.

their attack on Soviet Russia, the Ural Executive Committee has decided to execute you."[13] As the stunned tsar was trying to speak, Yurovsky repeated his statement and then shot and killed Nicholas.

The rest of the gunmen crowded into the small room and began firing. The tsarina and Princess Olga were killed immediately. The other princesses had sewn precious jewels into the linings of their gowns, and some of the bullets bounced off them and "ricocheted around the room."[14] One of the servants resisted. She had a stiff corset on, and the soldier who attacked her had difficulty penetrating it with his bayonet. Yurovsky saw that the tsarevich was still alive; he finished him off with two shots to the head.

When it was over, the executioners stripped the corpses of their jewelry and other valuables. They washed down the room, and then carried the corpses on stretchers to waiting trucks. The bodies were taken into the woods and burned. Acid was poured over the faces so that they could not be easily recognized. They were then taken to a deep mine and buried there. All this was done with the awareness that "the Russian people assigned miraculous powers to the remains of martyrs." The assassins wanted "to prevent a cult of the Romanovs" developing.[15]

It was, in every way, a horrible crime. Innocent people died. However, as Romanov chronicler Karl Shaw has observed, sympathy should not blot out the fact that Tsar Nicholas II "was one of the most sinister and cowardly royal despots of the century." The pogroms he had instigated by ordering the writing and distribution of that tissue of rabble-rousing, anti-Semitic lies, *The Protocols of the Learned Elders of Zion*, had added up to mass slaughter. The tsar had told his soldiers, "Don't skimp on the bullets."[16] A copy of *The Protocols* was found among his effects following his murder.

U.S. TROOPS IN RUSSIA

Pogroms were still occurring. Word reached the White Russians of the execution of the Romanov family, and they learned that the man in charge, Yurovsky, was a Jew. Some saw this as evidence of the Jewish plot outlined in *The Protocols*. White Russian armies were advancing at the start of autumn 1918, and "harsh treatment of non-Russian minorities, particularly the Jews," was often a matter of policy.[17] Red army soldiers also sometimes persecuted the Jews. In Russia, anti-Semitism crossed the battle lines.

The Whites' advances were in part due to outside help. On March 9, 1918, an Anglo-French force landed at Murmansk in northern Russia. Its purpose was to take the seaport and its major munitions depots before the Germans claimed them under the impending peace treaty. Once there, however, the Allied troops were reinforced to total 48,000 men. They took control of the Murmansk railway. The shelling of the city of Archangel by a British naval force, followed by the landing of troops there, secured that port for the Allies as well.

Meanwhile, the Japanese had seized Vladivostok. They were reinforced by British, French, and Italian troops. The total invasion force numbered 85,000. President Woodrow Wilson, who had broken off relations with the Bolshevik government, sent a small U.S. force to Vladivostok to assist the Czech Legion. Another U.S. force, under the command of a British general, was dispatched to Archangel to help the Czech Legion, "and organize a pro-Allied army."[18]

At first this support hindered the Red army's ability to drive back the Whites. The Communists feared a large-scale invasion by the Allies on the side of the White Russians. They feared an Allied advance on Moscow, and made plans to evacuate the capital city. There was concern about lack of organization in the Red army. Actually, however, the former tsarist officers appointed by Trotsky had created a well-trained and effective fighting force.

It was really the Red army's foes who were disorganized. Their aims differed from one another, and there was a lack of coordination among them. In western Siberia there were forces of 20,000 Czechs, 15,000 Cossacks, and 20,000 troops under separate White Russian leadership. There was no central command. In early September, the Reds scored a series of impressive successes, taking two major cities, Kazan and Simbirsk. These victories "marked a psychological turning of the tide" for both the Red army and the Communist leaders.[19]

Over the next two months, the Reds and the Whites continued winning battles and losing battles, with no decisive victory in sight. Then, in November 1918, Germany surrendered to the Allies. World War I was over, but the Russian civil war would drag on for another two years.

CHAPTER TEN

A WORLD
TO WIN

> Bolshevik: Comes the Revolution, we'll all have strawberries in our sour cream.
>
> Socialist: But I don't like strawberries in my sour cream.
>
> Bolshevik: Comes the Revolution, you'll like strawberries in your sour cream!
>
> Traditional quip of Socialist anti-Communists

The armistice of November 11, 1918, annulled the Treaty of Brest-Litovsk. By surrendering, Germany had given up all its World War I conquests, including those in Russia. Germany's defeat was total, and its troops in Ukraine and other areas of Russia had to pull out. They left behind a vast territory to be fought over by White and Red Russians for the next three years.

BIRTH OF THE COMINTERN

As the carnage mounted, Lenin persisted in his dream of worldwide revolution. He viewed the Spartacist rebellion in Germany in early January 1919 as its start. The Spartacist League, led by Karl Liebknecht and internationally renowned writer and scholar Rosa Luxemburg, had renamed itself the German Communist party. They agitated against elections and demanded a workers' government. They called on government workers to quit their jobs and join the revolution. They occupied newspaper offices. They fought pitched battles with police and soldiers. A correspondent reported "the bodies of hundreds of dead and wounded piled on sidewalks" as army troops crushed the uprising.[1] Liebknecht and Luxemburg were arrested. Liebknecht was shot by guards, allegedly while trying to escape. Luxemburg was seized by a mob, which beat her, shot her, and dumped her body in a canal.

In Moscow this was viewed as only the first chapter in the global revolution. Already, Zinoviev "had established the Communist Parties of Austria and Hungary."[2] Moscow-directed organizing campaigns were also proceeding in other countries. On March 2, 1919, an international Communist conference was held in Moscow. It was chaired by a five-member steering committee, which included Lenin and Yurovsky, who had supervised the murder of the royal family. Among the fifty-two delegates were representatives from France, Germany, Switzerland, Austria, Hungary, Finland, Poland, Ukraine, Armenia, and other countries. A Bolshevik proposal to create the Third Communist International was unanimously approved.

The First International had been established by Karl Marx and others in London in 1864, and dissolved in 1876 when the leftist parties could not agree on methods and goals. The Second International was founded in Paris in 1889, but broke up at the start of World War I when many of the members supported their countries' war efforts rather than the International's pacifist platform. The Third International, known as the Comintern, was formed to promote world revolution, but "functioned chiefly as an organ of Soviet control over the Communist movement" around the world.[3]

Zinoviev was appointed president of the Comintern. He announced that "the victory of Communism in the whole of Europe is totally inevitable," adding that "in a year the whole of Europe will be Communist." When that happened, Lenin added, there would be no need to listen to the "empty slogans of pure democracy."[4]

The world was listening. There was still Communist unrest in Germany and other countries. Bolshevik Béla Kun led a coalition of Communists and Social Democrats to seize power in Hungary. His announced aim was a dictatorship of the Hungarian proletariat. Kun's reign lasted only 133 days before it was toppled by royalist forces. Nevertheless, the stirring of workers' movements in other countries provoked those in power to take measures against all those they lumped together as Bolsheviks, whether or not they had any connection with Lenin's Comintern.

THE PALMER RAIDS

In the United States, politicians and industrialists grew increasingly fearful of the spread of bolshevism. Their fears were realized when, on June 2, 1919, a bomb shattered the homes of several top government officials in Washington. The men who set off the bomb were blown to bits. Among those whose homes were damaged was Attorney General A. Mitchell Palmer.

When race riots marked by violent clashes between African Americans and whites followed in Washington, D.C.; Norfolk, Virginia; and Chicago, where thirty-one people died, and more than five hundred were injured, officials assumed they were Bolshevik inspired. Railway workers went on strike and demanded that the government take over the railroads. In Boston, the police force went on strike. In Gary, Indiana, federal troops were called in when striking steelworkers attacked strikebreakers hired by the United States Steel Corporation. Palmer and others in government viewed these events as Communist inspired.

It was the start of what would become known as the Palmer Raids, a series of actions against organizations suspected of radical activity. These included six raids on the Union of Russian Workers in Manhattan followed by the arrest of 249 Russian aliens in December 1919. All were deported to Russia, including Emma Goldman, the famous radical whose stay there would convince her that Russian communism was a betrayal of the Socialist cause. A month later there was a nationwide roundup of foreign-born radicals. They were "held in seclusion for long periods of time, brought into secret hearings, and ordered deported." In Boston, six hundred people were seized in meeting halls or taken from their homes in the night. A troubled federal judge described the process: "The arrested aliens, in most instances perfectly quiet and harmless working people, many of them not long ago Russian peasants, were handcuffed in pairs, and then, for the purposes of transfer on trains and through the streets of Boston, chained together."[5]

By April, Palmer was charging that the railroad strike had been incited by "the International Communist Party, whose purpose is . . . to overthrow the government and establish a dictatorship."[6] Later that month Palmer said his agents had discovered a plot to kill American officials on May Day, an international workers' holiday. Like many of the charges leveled during the hysteria of those days, such plots were never proved.

A NEW RED ARMY

Fear that the Comintern was organizing revolutions in their countries pushed the United States and others to send supplies and troops to Russia. In 1919 foreign intervention bolstered the White Russians' campaign against the Reds. Admiral Aleksandr Kolchak, once commander of the tsar's Black Sea fleet, unified the White Russian army, the Czech Legion, and the Cossacks in western Siberia. His army was advancing into eastern Russia. Elated by its successes, the admiral adopted the title "Supreme Ruler of Russia."[7]

White Russian general Anton Denikin viewed this as an attempt to seize control of the counterrevolution. His forces were battling their way from Ukraine toward Moscow. Denikin was receiving arms and ammunition from the Allies through the seaport of Odessa, which was held by French forces. From the Baltic region, a White Russian army under General Nikolay Yudenich, who was also eager to establish himself as the dominant counterrevolutionary leader, was getting ready to march on St. Petersburg.

Red troops were falling back on all fronts. However, a massive effort was under way to organize a new army. Lenin had ordered the creation of a three-million-man force "to help the international workers' revolution." He had assigned the task to Trotsky, who once again turned to former tsarist officers to assemble and lead such an army. On November 23, 1918, "all officers under 50 and generals under 60 were ordered to register" for active duty. There were severe penalties for not registering. Trotsky threatened reprisals against "fathers, mothers, sisters, brothers, wives and children" of any officers who shirked their duty. Seventy-five thousand ex-tsarist officers served in the three-million-man Red army during the civil war—775 were generals.[8]

THE CIVIL WAR WINDS DOWN

In 1919 the new Red military won its first victories in Ukraine, but then suffered major defeats, which included the surrender of the Bolshevik first army. By August, General Denikin's forces had taken back all of Ukraine and were advancing toward Moscow. The Red government made plans to evacuate the capital.

Against Admiral Kolchak, on their eastern front, Communist forces were doing better. Not far from Archangel, White troops mutinied and joined the Reds. Kolchak's army was outnumbered and forced to retreat. In August, the U.S. government came to Kolchak's aid, authorizing arms shipments to Siberia for his troops.

By early October 1919, Cossacks under General Denikin were poised to take Moscow when Red troops, some of them led by Stalin, counterattacked. The Red force was so large that the Cossacks, and then the rest of Denikin's White army, were forced to retreat. They were driven all the way back to the Black Sea. Soldiers fleeing the Red cavalry converged on Novorossiysk, a Crimean port held by the Allies, and tried to force their way onto departing ships. The Reds held back because of a terrible typhus epidemic sweeping over Novorossiysk. Across the water, in Sebastopol, General Denikin resigned his command.

Meanwhile, General Yudenich, supported by a British fleet in the Gulf of Finland, was laying siege to St. Petersburg. On October 17, Lenin sent Trotsky there to take charge of the defense. What he found was a demoralized army, which had retreated in "shameful panic" and "senseless flight." Trotsky immediately replaced their commander. He addressed the troops, pointing out that they outnumbered the enemy. Then Trotsky mounted his horse and led them into battle. His "presence decisively affected the outcome." The Reds drove the Whites all the way back to the Estonian border, where they surrendered.[9]

By November, General Kolchak's army was in full flight in southern central Siberia. Outnumbered by the Red army, his supply lines cut, he gave up the city of Omsk and fled. The Reds took Omsk without a fight, and found warehouses filled with the Whites' guns and ammunition. According to an English observer, "tens of thousands of peaceful people" were also "rushing away from that Red Terror."[10]

Kolchak fled to Irkutsk, where a local government declared him "an enemy of the people." The Irkutsk Revolutionary Committee sentenced "the ex-Supreme Ruler, Admiral Kolchak . . . to be shot." On February 7, 1920, a poison pill concealed in his handkerchief was taken from Kolchak. At 4:00 A.M., he was executed. His body was pushed under the ice in the Ushakova River.[11]

During 1920, in the Crimea, a White Russian army was organized under the command of Count Peter Wrangel. They fought as a hit-and-run force until November, when a major battle took place. It ended with 30,000 White Russians killed and 40,000 captured. It was the last battle of the Russian civil war. On November 14, the war ended.

STALIN AND POLAND

The major Communist hero of the Russian civil war was Leon Trotsky, whose chief rival among Red leaders was Joseph Stalin. When Trotsky was awarded the Order of the Red Banner for saving St. Petersburg, a reason had to be found to honor Stalin as well. It was Lenin's policy to maintain a balance between the two men.

In January 1919, Stalin had been dispatched to the eastern front to report on the officers responsible for the defeat of Red forces by Kolchak. In May he went to Kronstadt, where he ordered the execution of sixty-seven naval officers "for disloyalty." Later in the year, he led forces that helped prevent the Whites' advance on Moscow. To some he was a hero, but to his critics, Stalin was a paranoid murderer prone to "seeing treachery and conspiracy where others saw inefficiency and muddle."[12]

Throughout the civil war, Stalin clashed with Trotsky over the ex-tsarist officers. They also disagreed about policy decisions. Matters came to a head in the spring of 1920. At this time there was a border dispute between Poland and Russia. Lenin wanted "to probe Europe with the bayonets of the Red Army" by invading Poland. Stalin eventually agreed, while Trotsky disagreed vehemently, believing that the Red army wasn't ready for such a venture.[13] Before Lenin could "probe," the Poles attacked in Ukraine. Despite his doubts, Trotsky took command and fought the Poles. Stalin was then inspecting the southwestern army group massed on what would be the southern part of the front against Poland. Lenin ordered him to detach a major part of these forces to join a march against Warsaw. Stalin refused. Instead he mounted an attack intended to capture the southern Polish city of Lvov. The Poles counterattacked, and the Reds suffered a major defeat. Stalin was recalled to Moscow and censured by Lenin.

Meanwhile, Trotsky's army was marching on Warsaw. Two retreating Polish armies regrouped and trapped the Red forces between them. By October 6, 1920, the Reds were beaten, and an armistice was signed. The treaty that followed gave Poland considerable Ukrainian and Belorussian territory.

FAMINE AND PURGE

In the wake of war, the Communists were faced with a more serious problem. Once the peasants realized they did not own the farms seized from the landowners and must turn over their produce to the government, they had balked at planting crops. The fighting had also disrupted crop production and interfered with transportation. As food lay rotting on railroad sidings, more than 18 million Russians were facing starvation. They were also facing a rapidly spreading cholera epidemic.

To retain power, Lenin was forced to betray the Bolshevik principle that had done away with private property. He introduced his New Economic Policy, which granted peasants ownership of their farms, plus the right to lease additional land, and sanctioned limited free enterprise. It allowed the peasants to plant, grow, and sell their crops at a profit in order to motivate them to feed the starving nation.

It came too late, however, to help the present situation. In August 1921, Lenin was forced to appeal to the capitalist nations to aid "their starving fellows in Russia."[14] Many responded, including the United States, which sent food for 20,000 children in St. Petersburg. This was followed by a major international relief effort headed by Allied administrator and future U.S. president Herbert Hoover.

Lenin then turned his attention to party politics. Calling criticism of his policies "petty-bourgeois deviations," he drove opposition factions out of the Russian Communist party. "Individuals guilty of such sins as corruption, incompetence, alcoholism, or opposition " were expelled. In all, party membership was cut from 700,000 "to around 400,000 in 1922." Wary of Trotsky's ambition, Lenin replaced those of his friends who held positions of power with a new group responsible to Stalin, who was appointed general secretary of the party in April 1922.[15]

A result of the civil war was famine for the peasants. These children, refugees in Russia, were photographed in October 1921.

Stalin immediately set about bringing the non-Russian states that had been part of the tsarist empire, and were now loosely federated with the Union of Soviet Socialist Republics (USSR), into line. These were territories with non-Russian ethnic populations, and non-Russian traditions. Some had been reconquered during the civil war, and some had welcomed the Red army as liberators from White landlord tyranny. Stalin used brutal measures to ensure their ties to the new federation, and to put them under the thumb of Bolshevik rule.

THE DAWN OF STALINISM

In May 1922, Lenin suffered the first in a series of strokes. Trotsky, "clearly the party's second ranking figure," should have replaced him.[16] However, the Central Committee of the Communist party passed him over in favor of a leadership troika (a Russian word meaning "a group of three") consisting of Zinoviev, longtime Bolshevik Lev Kamenev, and Stalin. They were charged with carrying out the antichurch campaign decreed by Lenin from his sickbed. The assets of all Russian religious institutions, particularly the Orthodox Church to which most Russians belonged, were to be seized by the state. If there was opposition, Lenin ordered "the execution of ringleaders among the clergy."[17]

Recovering briefly in the autumn of 1922, Lenin was critical of the troika, particularly Stalin. He attacked him for "his heavy-handed approach in forcing the non-Russian soviet republics to accept formal federation" in what was now the Union of Soviet Socialist Republics (USSR). He said that Stalin's rudeness "becomes intolerable in the office of General Secretary" and proposed "transferring Stalin from that position." In December, Lenin turned to Trotsky to depose Stalin. By now, however, Stalin had become too powerful. Zinoviev and Kamenev were afraid of him. Trotsky failed. In April 1923, Lenin had a final stroke, which left him helpless. That fall, Trotsky launched another attack on Stalin, and once again failed. Stalin now had control of the Communist party, and the party condemned Trotsky "for factionalism and anti-Marxist deviation."[18]

A crowd of thousands
in Red Square, Moscow, at Lenin's
funeral in January 1924

By the time Lenin died on January 21, 1924, Stalin was in absolute control of the party, the government, and the country. His thirty-year reign would be one of the most brutal in history. Millions of people would die by his orders. Most would be citizens of the Union of Soviet Socialist Republics.

AFTERWORD

The lesson of the Russian Revolution is that evil begets evil. Tsarist oppression of peasants and workers generated a rebellion as cruel as the tyranny that provoked it. Yet in the beginning, the ideas from which that rebellion sprang were rooted in the desire to make a better life for poor people, for peasants and workers who truly were exploited by those who owned the land, factories, and mines in which they toiled. The need for reform gave birth to the philosophy of socialism, and while that need could not be denied, the philosophy could be either constructively adapted to circumstances or twisted and distorted to secure, maintain, and exert power over millions of people.

Over the years, the reforms of democratic socialism have been incorporated into law by such programs as Social Security in the United States, socialized medicine in Great Britain, and free child care and other welfare programs in the Scandinavian nations and other countries. Some of these programs existed in Soviet Russia and still exist in other Communist countries. However, they exist as examples of ends justifying means, and the Communist means have been horrible.

Socialist reforms may have validity in a democratic system. They can never be valid under the repression of a totalitarian regime. It's a basic truth. No movement can free humanity from oppression by oppressing its fellow human beings.

CHRONOLOGY

1848 — January — Karl Marx and Friedrich Engels publish *The Communist Manifesto* in London.

1861 — Tsar Alexander II issues Emancipation Proclamation freeing the serfs.

1864 — First International established by Karl Marx and others.

1872 — March — *Das Kapital* published in Russia.

1876 — First International dissolved.

1881 — Tsar Alexander II assassinated.

1887 — Alexander Ulianov, brother of Vladimir Lenin, executed for attempting to kill Tsar Alexander III.

1889 — Second International founded in Paris.

1894–1901 — Five heads of state including U.S. President William McKinley are slain by anarchists.

1895 — Nicholas II becomes tsar.

1895 — Lenin exiled to Siberia for revolutionary activity.

1898 — Russian Social Democratic Labour party (Communists) holds First Party Congress in Minsk.

1902 — Anti-Semite Viacheslav Plehve becomes head of secret police.

1903 — Second Party Congress of Social Democrats held in Brussels; dominated by Lenin.
Revolutionist Joseph Stalin exiled to Siberia.
April 16 — Kishinev pogrom sets off chain reaction of pogroms across Russia.

1904—Tsarevich Alexis is born with hemophilia.

February 8—Japanese attack Russian fleet at Port Arthur; Russo-Japanese War begins.

March—Japanese destroy Russia's Pacific fleet at Vladivostok.

July—Secret Police Chief Plehve assassinated.

1905—Mystic Rasputin helps stop Alexis's bleeding and begins relationship with tsar and tsarina.

Unsuccessful revolution in Russia.

Sailors' mutiny aboard the *Potemkin* spreads to other ships in Odessa harbor.

October 30—October Manifesto, granting constitution and Duma, issued by Tsar Nicholas.

November 8—Black Hundreds' Odessa pogrom kills more than a thousand Jews.

1906—Bolsheviks boycott elections for first Duma, which tsar dissolves after 72 days.

August 12—Failed assassination attempt on new Prime Minister Petr Arkadevich Stolypin.

1907—Second Duma convened and dissolved by tsar after four months.

1911—U.S. Senate renounces 1832 treaty because of official anti-Semitism in Russia.

September 1—Assassin shoots Prime Minister Stolypin; he dies four days later.

1912—Prague Conference marks final break between Bolsheviks and Mensheviks.

Compromising letter from tsarina to Rasputin is leaked to press.

1913—Stalin arrested in St. Petersburg and again exiled to Siberia.

1914—June 28—Austrian Archduke Francis Ferdinand and wife assassinated.

July 28—World War I begins; on August 1, Germany declares war on Russia.

September 5—Treaty of London signed by Russia, France, and Great Britain pledges no separate peace with Germany.

1915—May—Russian casualties reach one million.

1916—June 5—Russian army launches successful major offensive.

December 16—Rasputin is assassinated by royalists.

1917—March—Rebellion in St. Petersburg sets up Provisional Government under Prince Lvov.

March 15—Tsar Nicholas II abdicates.

April 16—Lenin arrives at the Finland Station in St. Petersburg.

July—Bolsheviks try to seize control of the Provisional Government and fail.

July 20—Prince Lvov resigns; Aleksandr Kerensky named prime minister.

August—Promonarchy General Lavr Georgyevich Kornilov tries to take over Provisional Government, but fails.

November 7—Bloodless Bolshevik revolution succeeds in seizing control of the government; Kerensky flees.

November 15—Declaration of the Rights of People gives tsarist territories the option to set up independent states.

December 15—Armistice between Russia and Germany signed at Brest-Litovsk in violation of Treaty of London.

1918—January-May—Counterrevolution breaks out in several places.

March 3—Treaty of Brest-Litovsk gives Germany almost one-third of the Russian empire.

June—Stalin reorganizes Tsaritsyn garrison and clashes with Leon Trotsky over using tsarist officers.

July—Socialist Revolutionaries (SRs) rebel against Bolsheviks; Lenin severely wounded by assassination attempt; mass retaliations leave 1,300 dead.

July 16—Tsar Nicholas II, his wife, son, four daughters, three servants, and physician are brutally executed.

November 11—Germany surrenders; World War I ends; Treaty of Brest-Litovsk annulled.

1919—Civil war rages in Russia.

General Aleksandr Kolchak's army in Siberia is defeated by Reds; Kolchak taken prisoner; later executed.

January—Spartacist rebellion in Germany put down.

March 2—Third Communist International (Comintern) created.

June 2—Bombing in Washington, D.C., provokes anti-Bolshevik hysteria and Palmer Raids.

October—Moscow under siege by Cossacks; Red army counterattacks; drives army of General Anton Denekin all the way to the Black Sea; Denekin resigns his command; siege of St. Petersburg by General Nikolay Yudenich's White army is broken by Trotsky-led Red forces; Whites flee, then surrender at Estonian border.

1920—Lenin introduces New Economic Policy giving peasants land ownership.

White army organized by Count Peter Wrangel.

April—Poland invades Russian Ukraine; forces commanded by Stalin defeated by Poles at Lvov.

October 6—Trotsky army marching on Warsaw is defeated by Poles; armistice is signed; peace terms give Poles considerable Russian and Belorussian territory.

November 14—Count Wrangel defeated by Red army; Russian civil war ends.

1921 — Famine in Russia.

August — Lenin appeals to capitalist nations for aid; U.S. President Herbert Hoover heads international aid effort.

1922 — Lenin purges opposition, cutting Russian Communist party by 300,000 members.

Antichurch campaign seizes assets of all Russian religious institutions; clergy who oppose are ordered executed.

April — Stalin appointed general secretary of Russian Communist party.

May — Lenin suffers first stroke; Trotsky passed over in favor of leadership troika of Grigori Zinoviev, Lev Kamenev, and Stalin.

Fall — Lenin briefly recovers from stroke, criticizes troika, and proposes removing Stalin as general secretary.

1924 — January 21 — Lenin dies; Stalin begins his brutal thirty-year dictatorship.

CHAPTER NOTES

CHAPTER ONE

Opening quote: Nikolai Kekrasov, *Who Is Happy in Russia?* in *Bartlett's Familiar Quotations: Fourteenth Edition* (Boston: Little, Brown and Company, 1968), p. 710a.

1. *Encyclopedia Britannica: Handy Volume Issue*, Vol. 23 (New York: The Encyclopedia Britannica Company, 1911), p. 870.

2. *Encyclopedia Britannica: Handy Volume Issue*, p. 869.

3. *Encyclopedia Britannica: Handy Volume Issue*, p. 872.

4. Richard Pipes, *The Russian Revolution* (New York: Alfred A. Knopf, 1990), p. 347.

5. *Encyclopedia Britannica: Handy Volume Issue*, Vol. 23 (New York: The Encyclopedia Britannica Company, 1911), p. 904.

6. *Encyclopedia Britannica: Handy Volume Issue*, p. 905.

7. Orlando Figes, *A People's Tragedy: A History of the Russian Revolution*, (New York: Viking, 1997) p. 48.

8. Pipes, p. 60.

9. Pipes, p. 142.

10. Pipes, p. 142.

11. Pipes, p. 343.

12. Author uncredited. *V. I. Lenin* (NYPL Electronic Resources: Biography Resource Center, *Historic World Leaders*, Gale Research, 1994), p. 2.

13. *V. I. Lenin*, p. 3.

14. Pipes, p. 364.

15. Pipes, p. 81.

16. Barbara W. Tuchman, *The Proud Tower* (Toronto: Bantam Books, 1985), p. 72.

17. *Encyclopedia Britannica: Handy Volume Issue*, p. 876.

18. Tuchman, pp. 274–275.

19. Pipes, pp. 59–60.

20. *Encyclopedia Britannica,* Vol. I (Chicago: Encyclopedia Britannica, 1984), p. 226.

21. *Encyclopedia Britannica,* Vol. IV, p.1015.

22. Pipes, p. 224.

CHAPTER TWO

Opening quote: Barbara W. Tuchman, *The Proud Tower* (Toronto: Bantam Books, 1985), p. 130.

1. Orlando Figes, *A People's Tragedy: A History of the Russian Revolution* (New York: Viking, 1997), p. 28; author uncredited, *Rasputin* (Cambridge: Compton's Interactive Encyclopedia, 1998).

2. Figes, p. 29.

3. *Rasputin.*

4. Figes, p. 29.

5. Figes, p. 30.

6. Figes, p. 30.

7. Richard Pipes, *The Russian Revolution* (New York: Alfred A. Knopf, 1990), p. 9.

8. Pipes, pp. 10–11.

9. Max I. Dimont, *Jews, God and History* (New York: New American Library, 1962), p. 321.

10. *Chronicle of the 20th Century* (Mount Kisco, NY: Chronicle Publications, 1987), p. 51.

11. *Chronicle of the 20th Century,* p. 51.

12. Howard M. Sachar, *A History of the Jews in America* (New York: Alfred A. Knopf, 1992), p. 131.

13. *Encyclopedia Britannica: Handy Volume Issue,* Vol. 23 (New York: The Encyclopedia Britannica Company, 1911), p. 874.

14. Sachar, p. 131.

15. *Chronicle of the 20th Century,* p. 61.

16. *Chronicle of the 20th Century,* p. 61.

17. Pipes, p. 20.

18. Figes, p. 173.

19. *Chronicle of the 20th Century,* pp. 73–74.

20. *Chronicle of the 20th Century,* p. 81.

21. Figes, p. 191.

22. *Encyclopedia Britannica,* Vol. VIII (Chicago: Encyclopedia Britannica, 1984), p. 729.

CHAPTER THREE

Opening quote: Karl Marx and Frederick Engels, *The Communist Manifesto: A Modern Edition* (London: Verso, 1998), p. 33.

1. Dmitri Volkogonov, *Autopsy for an Empire: The Seven Leaders Who Built the Soviet Regime* (New York: The Free Press, 1998), p. xviii.
2. *Encyclopedia Britannica*, Vol. II (Chicago: Encyclopedia Britannica, 1984), p. 549.
3. Author uncredited. *Karl Marx* (NYPL Electronic Resources: Biography Resource Center, *Historic World Leaders*, Gale Research, 1994), p. 2.
4. *Encyclopedia Britannica*, p. 549.
5. Tom Morris, *Philosophy for Dummies* (New York, IDG Books, 1999), p. 332.
6. *Encyclopedia Britannica*, p. 549.
7. *Karl Marx*, p. 3.
8. *Karl Marx*, p. 3.
9. *Encyclopedia Britannica*, Vol. IV, p. 1020.
10. *Encyclopedia Britannica*, Vol. III, p. 518.
11. *Karl Marx*, p. 4.
12. Marx and Engels, pp. 34–35.
13. *Karl Marx*, p. 4.
14. Marx and Engels, p. 77.
15. *Encyclopedia Britannica*, Vol. II, p. 550.
16. *Bakunin, Mikhail*, Compton's Interactive Encyclopedia, 1998.
17. *Encyclopedia Britannica*, Vol. II, p. 552.
18. *Encyclopedia Britannica*, Vol. II, p. 551.
19. Orlando Figes, *A People's Tragedy: A History of the Russian Revolution* (New York: Viking, 1997), p. 139.
20. Figes, p. 139.

CHAPTER FOUR

Opening quote: Orlando Figes, *A People's Tragedy: A History of the Russian Revolution* (New York: Viking, 1997), p. 223.
1. Figes, p. 149.
2. *Encyclopedia Britannica*, Vol. II (Chicago: Encyclopedia Britannica, 1984), p. 132.
3. Alan Bullock, *Hitler and Stalin: Parallel Lives* (New York: Alfred A. Knopf, 1992), pp. 28–29.
4. Figes, p. 153.
5. *Encyclopedia Britannica*, Vol. XVI, p. 66.
6. Richard Pipes, *The Russian Revolution* (New York: Alfred A. Knopf, 1990), p. 158.
7. Figes, p. 201.
8. Figes, pp. 221, 223.
9. Pipes, p. 178.
10. *Encyclopedia Britannica*, Vol. XVI, p. 67.
11. Figes, p. 34.
12. Figes, p. 31.

13. Figes, p. 227.

14. Pipes, p. 188.

CHAPTER FIVE

Opening quote: John Gunther (quoting Stalin), *Soviet Russia Today in Bartlett's Familiar Quotations: Fourteenth Edition* (Boston: Little, Brown and Company, 1968), p. 954b.

1. Richard Pipes, *The Russian Revolution* (New York: Alfred A. Knopf, 1990), p. 375.

2. Pipes, p. 375.

3. Author uncredited. *Leon Trotsky* (NYPL Electronic Resources: Biography Resource Center, *Historic World Leaders*, Gale Research, 1994), p. 3.

4. *Encyclopedia Britannica*, Vol. XVIII (Chicago: Encyclopedia Britannica, 1984), pp. 717–718.

5. Author uncredited. *Grigori Evseevich Zinoviev* (NYPL Electronic Resources: Biography Resource Center, *Historic World Leaders*, Gale Research, 1994), p. 1.

6. Pipes, p. 378.

7. Dmitri Volkogonov, *Autopsy for an Empire: The Seven Leaders Who Built the Soviet Regime* (New York: The Free Press, 1998), p. 86.

8. Alan Bullock, *Hitler and Stalin: Parallel Lives* (New York: Alfred A. Knopf, 1992), p. 5.

9. Volkogonov, p. 85.

10. Bullock, p. 27.

11. Bullock, p. 7.

12. Volkogonov, p. 86.

13. Bullock, pp. 32–33.

14. Bullock, p. 35.

15. Bullock, p. 38.

CHAPTER SIX

Opening quote: Richard Pipes, *The Russian Revolution* (New York: Alfred A. Knopf, 1990), p. 378.

1. Barbara W. Tuchman, *The Proud Tower* (Toronto: Bantam Books, 1985), p. 525.

2. Tuchman, p. 527.

3. Tuchman, p. 280.

4. Pipes, p. 196.

5. Karl Shaw, *Royal Babylon: The Alarming History of European Royalty* (New York: Broadway Books, 2001), p. 180.

6. *Encyclopedia Britannica*, Vol. XIX (Chicago: Encyclopedia Britannica, 1984), p. 945.

7. Author uncredited. *Alexander Kerensky* (NYPL Electronic Resources: Biography Resource Center, *Historic World Leaders*, Gale Research, 1994), p. 3.

8. *Chronicle of the 20th Century* (Mount Kisco, NY: Chronicle Publications, 1987), p. 188.

9. Pipes, p. 224.

10. Orlando Figes, *A People's Tragedy: A History of the Russian Revolution* (New York: Viking, 1997), p. 33.

11. Figes, p. 32.

12. Pipes, p. 224.

13. Pipes, p. 233.

14. Figes, p. 113.

15. Pipes, p. 252.

16. Figes, p. 277.

17. Figes, p. 284.

CHAPTER SEVEN

Opening quote: Orlando Figes, *A People's Tragedy: A History of the Russian Revolution* (New York: Viking, 1997), p. 283.

1. Figes, p. 283.

2. Karl Shaw, *Royal Babylon: The Alarming History of European Royalty* (New York: Broadway Books, 2001), p. 183.

3. Richard Pipes, *The Russian Revolution* (New York: Alfred A. Knopf, 1990), p. 265.

4. Pipes, p. 265.

5. Pipes, p. 265.

6. Pipes, p. 267.

7. Figes, p. 307.

8. Figes, p. 308.

9. Figes, p. 313.

10. Figes, p. 323.

11. Figes, p. 337.

12. Pipes, p. 313.

CHAPTER EIGHT

Opening quote: John Reed, *Ten Days That Shook the World* (London: Penguin Books, 1977), p. 69.

1. Richard Pipes, *The Russian Revolution* (New York: Alfred A. Knopf, 1990), p. 390.

2. Brian Crozier, *The Rise and Fall of the Soviet Empire* (Rocklin, CA: Prima Publishing, 1999), p. 8.

3. *Chronicle of the 20th Century* (Mount Kisco, NY: Chronicle Publications, 1987), p. 218.

4. Orlando Figes, *A People's Tragedy: A History of the Russian Revolution* (New York: Viking, 1997), p. 387.

5. Figes, p. 387.

6. *Chronicle of the 20th Century,* p. 219.

7. Pipes, pp. 422, 427.

8. Pipes, pp. 432–433.

9. Figes, pp. 442–443.

10. Figes, p. 444.

11. *Encyclopedia Britannica,* Vol. XVI (Chicago: Encyclopedia Britannica, 1984), p. 69.

12. *Encyclopedia Britannica,* Vol. XVI, p. 69.

13. Author uncredited. *Grigori Evseevich Zinoviev* (NYPL Electronic Resources: Biography Resource Center, *Historic World Leaders,* Gale Research, 1994), p. 2.

14. Reed, p. 71.

15. Reed, p. 73.

16. Reed, p. 89.

CHAPTER NINE

Opening quote: Alan Bullock, *Hitler and Stalin: Parallel Lives* (New York: Alfred A. Knopf, 1992), p. 60.

1. *Encyclopedia Britannica,* Vol. XVI (Chicago: Encyclopedia Britannica, 1984), p. 69.

2. *Chronicle of the 20th Century* (Mount Kisco, NY: Chronicle Publications, 1987), p. 224.

3. *Chronicle of the 20th Century,* p. 224.

4. *Encyclopedia Britannica,* Vol. II, p. 257.

5. Bullock, p. 62.

6. *Encyclopedia Britannica* Vol. XIX, p. 958.

7. Brian Crozier, *The Rise and Fall of the Soviet Empire* (Rocklin, CA: Prima Publishing, 1999), p. 12.

8. Bullock, p. 61.

9. Crozier, p. 20.

10. Bullock, p. 98.

11. Bullock, p. 99.

12. Orlando Figes, *A People's Tragedy: A History of the Russian Revolution* (New York: Viking, 1997), p. 639.

13. Karina Fielderova, "Czar Nicholas II Assassinated" in the *Moscow Times,* July 18, 1918, p. 1.
   <hiltonheadhigh.com/coolwork/newspapers/nicholas/nicholas.htm>

14. Karina Fielderova.

15. Richard Pipes, *The Russian Revolution* (New York: Alfred A. Knopf, 1990), p. 777.

16. Karl Shaw, *Royal Babylon: The Alarming History of European Royalty* (New York: Broadway Books, 2001), pp. 6, 185.

17. *Encyclopedia Britannica,* Vol. XVI, p. 70.

18. Pipes, p. 657.

19. Pipes, p. 660.

CHAPTER TEN

Opening quote: *Chronicle of the 20th Century* (Mount Kisco, NY: Chronicle Publications, 1987), p. 246.

1. *Chronicle of the 20th Century,* p. 246.

2. Dmitri Volkogonov, *Autopsy for an Empire: The Seven Leaders Who Built the Soviet Regime* (New York: The Free Press, 1998), p. 45.

3. *Encyclopedia Britannica,* Vol. V (Chicago: Encyclopedia Britannica, 1984), p. 384.

4. Volkogonov, p. 46.

5. Howard Zinn, *A People's History of the United States* (New York: Harper & Row, 1980), p. 366.

6. *Chronicle of the 20th Century,* p. 265.

7. Brian Crozier, *The Rise and Fall of the Soviet Empire* (Rocklin, CA: Prima Publishing, 1999), p. 26.

8. Richard Pipes, *Russia Under the Bolshevik Regime* (New York: Alfred A. Knopf, 1993), pp. 51–52.

9. Pipes, p. 124.

10. Pipes, p. 115.

11. Pipes, pp. 116, 118.

12. Alan Bullock, *Hitler and Stalin: Parallel Lives* (New York: Alfred A. Knopf, 1992), p. 101.

13. Bullock, p. 101.

14. *Chronicle of the 20th Century,* p. 282.

15. *Encyclopedia Britannica,* Vol. XVI, p. 72.

16. *Encyclopedia Britannica,* Vol. XVI, p. 72.

17. Volkogonov, p. 81.

18. *Encyclopedia Britannica,* Vol. XVI, p. 72.

AFTERWORD

Opening quote: Howard Zinn, *A People's History of the United States* (New York: Harper & Row, 1980), p. 365.

GLOSSARY

anarchism—the theory that formal government of any kind is unnecessary

April Thesis—Lenin's demand that rule over Russia be transferred from the Provisional Government to the workers' soviets

Black Hundreds—antirevolutionaries who slaughtered those they considered agitators and who carried out pogroms

Bloody Sunday (January 9, 1905)—the day on which tsarist troops killed five hundred marchers during a peaceful demonstration for improved working conditions

Bolsheviks—literally "the majority," they would claim to represent the workers of the world; also an early name for Communists

bourgeoisie—owners of the means of production and employers of wage laborers

capitalism—private ownership and free trade for profit

civil war—the counterrevolution by White Russians following the Bolshevik takeover

Comintern (The Third International)—Communist organization formed to promote policies of world revolution

communism—ownership of all property by the community as a whole

Communist Manifesto—pamphlet in which Karl Marx and Friedrich Engels spelled out the aims of communism

constitutional monarchy—a democratically elected government headed by a monarch; patterned after that of Great Britain

Cossacks—tsarist cavalry who brutalized peasants and conducted pogroms

Council of Ministers—appointed cabinet of advisers to the tsar

Council of People's Commissars—cabinet made up of the heads of various branches of the Bolshevik government with Lenin as chairman

Czechoslovak Legion—volunteers who joined the tsarist army to fight the Germans and later fought the Red army

Das Kapital—Karl Marx's three-volume study of capitalism

Declaration of the Rights of Peoples—Bolshevik proclamation giving territories of the former tsarist empire the right to secede from Russia and set up independent nations

dialectic—the process by which tension and conflict result in human progress

dialectical materialism—the theory that if people's economic situation is changed, their ideas will change

Dictatorship of the Proletariat—rule *by* the common people, distorted to become rule *of* the common people by Communist despots

Duma—Russian parliament

emancipation proclamation—1861 document freeing the serfs from bondage

Ice March—major retreat by White Russian army

Imperial Russia—vast territory ruled by the tsar

industrial revolution—the change in social and economic conditions resulting from the replacement of hand tools by machine and power tools

intelligentsia—those regarding themselves as the intellectual, or learned, class

Kadets (Constitutional Democrats)—centrists who fought for a constitutional monarchy in the Duma

Marxism—system of economics developed by Karl Marx

Masonic Order—secret fraternal organization with chapters throughout the world

Mensheviks—literally "the minority," they were members of the Russian Social Democratic Labour party who opposed extremist Bolshevik programs

monarchist—one who favored a supreme Romanov ruler

Narodnaia Volia (People's Will)—Russian anarchist revolutionary group that believed in assassination as a political tool

New Economic Policy—Lenin's edict granting peasants ownership of land and right to sell produce

Palmer Raids—Post–World War I actions and deportations by U.S. Justice Department against individuals and organizations suspected of radical activity

pogrom—raids in which peasants and Cossacks robbed, raped, and murdered Jews

proletariat—workers; those whose only capital is their labor

Protocols of the Learned Elders of Zion—tract written at tsar's order to stir up anti-Semitism

Provisional Government—body that ruled Russia between abdication of Tsar Nicholas II and Bolshevik takeover

Red—Communist

Romanovs—the ruling tsarist family of Imperial Russia

Russian Social Democratic Labour party — 1898 organization that would evolve into the Communist party

Schlieffen Plan — German strategy for a two-front war

serf — a peasant bound to the landowner by conditions of feudal servitude; a virtual slave

Social Democrats — middle-of-the-road reform party

Socialist — one who believes in modified reforms based on Marxist principles

Socialist Revolutionary party (SR) — extreme radical Russian organization to the left of the bolsheviks, and leaning toward anarchism

soviet — council of workers

Soviet of Workers' Deputies — body elected by soviets to help form a Provisional Government to replace the tsar

Spartacist League — original name of the German Communist party

Stolypin's neckties — hangmen's nooses named after the ruthless tsarist prime minister

Temporary Committee of the Duma — members appointed by the Duma to work with the Soviet of Workers' Deputies to form a Provisional Government

troika — three-person leadership group

Trudoviki (Labor Group) — centrist Socialist party represented by Kerensky in the fourth Duma

tsar — Romanov ruler of Imperial Russia

tsarevich — son of the tsar, and heir to the throne

tsarina — wife of the tsar

Union of Soviet Socialist Republics (USSR) — collection of nations making up Soviet Russia

United Nobility — right-wing organization of aristocrats opposed to reform

Whites — anti-Communist Russians

FOR MORE INFORMATION

Bullock, Alan. *Hitler and Stalin: Parallel Lives*. New York: Alfred A. Knopf, 1992.

Crozier, Brian *The Rise and Fall of the Soviet Empire*. Rocklin, CA: Prima Publishing, 1999.

Dimont, Max I. *Jews, God and History*. New York: New American Library, 1962.

Figes, Orlando. *A People's Tragedy: A History of the Russian Revolution*. New York: Viking, 1997.

Hosking, Geoffrey, *Russia and the Russians: A History*. Boston: Harvard, 2001.

Lawrence, Sir John. *A History of Russia*. New York: Meridian, 1993.

MacKenzie, David. *A History of Russia and the Soviet Union*. Homewood, IL: Dorset Press, 1977.

Marx, Karl, and Frederick Engels. *The Communist Manifesto: A Modern Edition*. London: Verso, 1998.

Massie, Robert K. *Nicholas and Alexandra*. New York: Ballantine Books, 2000.

Pipes, Richard. *Russia Under the Bolshevik Regime*. New York: Alfred A. Knopf, 1993.

Pipes, Richard. *The Russian Revolution*. New York: Alfred A. Knopf, 1990.

Shaw, Karl. *Royal Babylon: The Alarming History of European Royalty*. New York: Broadway Books, 2001.

Tuchman, Barbara W. *The Proud Tower.* Toronto: Bantam Books, 1985.

Volkogonov, Dmitri. *Autopsy for an Empire: The Seven Leaders Who Built the Soviet Regime.* New York: The Free Press, 1998.

INTERNET SITES

Joseph Stalin Reference Archive: 1879–1953
    <www.marxists.org/reference/archive/stalin/>

Czar Nicholas II Assassinated in "Newspapers from the Past," a project of Hilton Head High School
    <www.hiltonheadhigh.com/coolwork/newspapers/nicholas/nicholas.htm>

Karl Marx and Friedrich Engels: *The Communist Manifesto* (1848)
    <www.wsu.edu:8080/~wldciv/world_civ_reader/world_civ_reader_2/marx.html>

Military History: Russian Revolution (1917–1921) War, Peace and Security Guide, Information Resource Centre, Canadian Forces College
    <www.cfcsc.dnd.ca/links/milhist/rusrev.html>
Russian Revolution in Dates
    <www.barnsdle.demon.co.uk/russ/datesr.html>

History & Culture of Russia: The Path to Revolution
    <www.interknowledge.com/russia/rushis06.htm>

Vladimir Lenin
    <members.nbci.com/1870/rus/>

INDEX